What people

Empathy i

Jerry Hyde has traveled deep within himself as well as to the farthest horizons to understand how harm comes to us and how it may be healed. There is a profound, urgent wisdom in his work that is carried along almost pell-mell by his enthusiasm for humanity and for life. I loved it.

Sebastian Junger, author of *The Perfect Storm, Korengal, War, Tribe*, and director of Which Way is the Front Line From Here? and Restrepo

Jerry Hyde is a unique human being, life experimenter, and psychotherapist. I greatly admire what he's been doing, and his new work is a wonderful introduction to what makes him one of a kind.

Luke Rhinehart, author of *The Dice Man, Whim, The Search for the Dice Man, The Book of the Die*

A pinch of history, a dash of rock 'n' roll, a tablespoon of philosophy, cups of psychology and heaping bowlfuls of wisdom; this book is a radical recipe for diving deep into your soul. The seemingly simple self-directed questions that punctuate each chapter prove surprisingly potent. Jerry is honest, brave, powerfully vulnerable, direct; he won't coddle, but his care is evident on every page. Ingest this book, it will transform you.

Melissa Unger, author of *Gag*, founder of Seymour Projects

Empathy for the Devil

Make your demons work for you.
Without selling your soul.

Empathy for the Devil

Make your demons work for you.
Without selling your soul.

Jerry Hyde

BOOKS

Winchester, UK
Washington, USA

JOHN HUNT PUBLISHING

First published by O-Books, 2021
O-Books is an imprint of John Hunt Publishing Ltd., 3 East St., Alresford,
Hampshire SO24 9EE, UK
office@jhpbooks.com
www.johnhuntpublishing.com
www.o-books.com

For distributor details and how to order please visit the 'Ordering' section on our website.

Text copyright: Jerry Hyde 2020

ISBN: 978 1 78904 731 8
978 1 78904 732 5 (ebook)
Library of Congress Control Number: 2020942296

A CIP catalogue record for this book is available from the British Library.

Design: Stuart Davies

UK: Printed and bound by CPI Group (UK) Ltd, Croydon, CR0 4YY
Printed in North America by CPI GPS partners

We operate a distinctive and ethical publishing philosophy in
all areas of our business, from our global network of authors to
production and worldwide distribution.

Contents

Other Books by this Author

The Book of Sin: How to Save the World. A Practical Guide
ISBN 978-1-78535-693-3

Play From Your Fucking Heart: A Somewhat Twisted Escape
Plan for People Who Usually Hate Self-Help Books
ISBN 978-1-78279-408-0

Bladesville
ISBN 978-1-84728-2-446

Dreamachine
ASIN B006WE499Q

For Truc-Mai

All this power will I give thee, and the glory of them: for that is delivered unto me; and to whomsoever I will I give it.
Luke: Chapter 4, Verse 6

ΚΑΤΑ ΤΟΝ ΔΑΙΜΟΝΑ ΕΑΥΤΟΥ
(ACCORDING TO HIS OWN DAIMON)

Inscription on Jim Morrison's grave

Here we go...

Have you ever been in one of those *Tesla* sports cars?

They have two acceleration modes – *Sport* or *Insane*.

If you're foolhardy enough to press option 2, and let's face it, who *isn't*, you'll be propelled from 0-60 in just over three seconds.

When smoked, the venom from the Sonoran Desert toad has a similar effect.

Within moments of inhalation you're rushing like a bastard through a blizzard of fractals that usher in a near death experience as very quickly you come to the understanding that, like it or not – you're going *in...*

To the light.

First time it took me a while before I realised the person on the other side of the room groaning like they were dying from a serious head wound was me.

A great many people report when under the influence of 5-MeO-DMT – for this is the active ingredient of the dried venom which is widely considered the most powerful psychedelic known to man or beast – they experience a deep and profound bliss state, a period of oneness and pure love, total, transcendental ego death and for this reason 5-MeO is often called the God particle.

Wasn't quite like that for me.

No – I'd say it was more like the single most intense experience of absolute, unadulterated, pure raw emotional pain *imaginable?*

It lasted maybe... 10 minutes? 15? Impossible to say really – time, space, here, there, up, down, now, then, *me...* all had all become rather vague. I was adrift in an eternity of darkness, at the heart of which throbbed a formless mass of incredible density and a voice was saying, *this is your pain. This is your pain; it has always been here.*

It will always be here.

Some is yours and some is others.

It is not to be cured, nor avoided, there is no shame, it does not make you weak nor less than, this is what is at the heart of all men – you are fragile, you are sensitive, you are vulnerable, these are not traits that belong to the feminine...

These are the qualities men have denied.

A distractingly beautiful Spanish woman dosed me – one should never fly solo on these missions – she had a day job in the city and carried herself with a mystical and somewhat reptilian impassivity which hinted she was perhaps one of the alien shape-shifters I'd heard so much about on YouTube, a notion that in my whacked-out state seemed all the more plausible.

Are you ready?

I'd been semi aware of her refilling the pipe and so, with not inconsiderable effort, I unglued myself from the floor...

And pressed the insane button once again.

Second time round the groaning was louder, I was conscious of her supporting my body as I vomited into a bucket but – who cared? It wasn't my body anymore. I was lost in a swirling vortex of geometric patterns, a trillion stars collapsing ever inwards on themselves as they exploded into infinite space, a colourless universe at the heart of which was a shapeless mass of dark matter, the pain even more intense now taking me to the edge of panic, body panting as might a rabid dog on a searing hot day and somehow, somewhere beyond torment, beyond ordeal, beyond crucifixion there was calm and understanding that, like some kind of Victorian adventurer, I had journeyed to the epicentre of my own darkness and found the spring from whence all pain flowed and a voice was saying *much of the world's problems are because men have learned to hide their frailty and vulnerability, but removing the mask is the way forward, this...*

Is the new masculinity.

And suddenly everything was okay.

This book... is a *shadow* book.

If you came here hoping for positive affirmations or creative visualisations, I gotta tell you right now – they're pretty thin on the ground. I mean, there *are* some transformational exercises, but they're kinda shady and don't involve dolphins or crystals... Personal growth isn't – and *shouldn't* be – nice, it's not about dream catchers, gong baths or djembe abuse – it's about going to the places most of us have successfully avoided throughout our lives, facing our demons and taking responsibility for whatever we find in the dark recesses of our being.

Take a look at the world around you.

Like it or not, there's never been a better time to go into the very heart of your own darkness, and I suggest you do just that – while you still have the choice.

Most therapies will encourage you to look at what a *good* person you are, in order to boost your self-esteem. I won't. I want you to recognise what a total asshole you can be.

In order to boost your self-esteem.

Because unless you acknowledge and own your own shadow, it doesn't matter how much people adore you, you'll always be thinking, *but if you really knew who I was – you wouldn't love me...*

The world and the human race are on the edge of a precipice and it may be too late to step back from the brink. The challenge on an individual level is to take responsibility for ourselves, for how we manage our pain, for our impact on the world and its inhabitants, for our own decisions and experiences, to not be one of the herd but to be conscious, because whilst it may feel easier to just *follow orders*, as we have seen in the not-too-distant past and shall see as this book progresses...

That way lays Armageddon...

Much of whether we are at the dusk or dawn of our species' existence is out of our hands, but on a personal level I believe we all must do whatever we can to evolve, because that's where real, immediate, tangible change can take place – inside each and every soul who's brave enough to go into their own intimate underworld, to ultimately emerge on the other side singed but in possession of superpowers.

Because all superheroes are freaks, for that is what evolution really is – *mutation*. And seeing as you've chosen to read this, chances are, in the rhetoric of 1960s counterculture, you're a freak, and freak power – that being the collective revolution by misfits, oddballs, outsiders and weirdos – may well save the world, given that the conventional old school patriarchal fucks running this planet have brought us to the perimeters of extinction.

The last 75 years has been sold to us as the Space Age, an era of ease, an instant plastic era of simplicity, efficiency, automation and abundance, and we've all been complicit in gobbling up this smorgasbord of consumerist delights, and now we're paying the price as the post-World War II era collapses before our frenzied eyes like a cold deck of cards.

As with everything, however – it's not all bad. Within this biblical landscape of plague, mass confinement, brutality, death, fire, pestilence, oppression, deception, corruption, white supremacy, riots, dictators and toppled statues is an opportunity for *real* change.

At the time of writing I've been a therapist for 25 years, and at no point has anyone ever walked into my practice room and said, *actually y'know what? I feel fantastic – I'm on top of the world...* No, they come in when they're heartbroken, destroyed, on their knees, lost, abandoned, alone.

In unbearable pain.

We, as a species, are complacent motherfuckers. It's only when we're hurting that we tend to evolve.

And right now, the world is *really* hurting.

This book has itself been painful; the hardest of anything I've ever written, it twisted and turned and refused to be pinned down or contained. Like some kind of wild, Comanche colt it dragged me around the prairie clinging on to its back – and often falling off – refusing to be tamed. Of course we are fools if we imagine that it is us who write books; we don't, they use us like incubi, they are demons and we the portal through which they arrive in their own damn good time, bursting forth from our chests when we least expect it.

It took me to places I never imagined, it broke me and changed me profoundly. I hope it does the same for you – and by *break*, I mean to shatter the calcified crust of your outdated persona to get to the hidden parts of your being so that you can thrive and grow.

I've been called, perhaps jokingly, perhaps not – the most dangerous therapist in the world, and as such I've worked with an incredibly diverse crowd of people over the years – mercenaries, murderers, murder victims, psychopaths, musicians, artists, rapists, rape victims, paedophiles, rock stars, actors, authors, celebrities, suicides, high achievers, abject failures, sex addicts, drug addicts, porn addicts, shopaholics, workaholics, alcoholics, psychedelic explorers, wife beaters, shoe sniffers and piss club aficionados.

And I'm the only therapist I ever heard of who worked with a ventriloquist and his dummy.

I've done marriage guidance, sex therapy, anger management, violence prevention, creativity coaching, I've buried people alive, given them Class A narcotics (allegedly), starved people for days, kept them awake for weeks at a time, but none of this is what makes me the most dangerous therapist in the world.

What makes me – and *any* half-decent therapist – dangerous, is my understanding that true transformation is a process of death and rebirth, death and rebirth, death and rebirth, a constant never-ending cycle of destruction and creation, shattering and rebuilding, chaos and order with no objective other than to constantly be in a state of evolution.

And to those with a rigid sense of who they believe themselves to be...

That's fucking dangerous.

Because I've got some good news and some bad news for you – there is no true self.

We are *all* legion.

Within each and every person is a huge cast of ever-expanding characters, some positive, some less so. They're visible in our language – *he has a nasty side; there's a part of me I don't like very much; he's a monster when he's drunk...* just some of the ways we refer to the negative, destructive, baser aspects of ourselves that with effort can be transmuted from demons – into daimōns.

This is a crucial point – there's a *big* difference between a demon and a daimōn. The word demon comes from the Latin word *daemonium* which means lesser or evil spirit, a dark, malevolent force that – like it or not – each of us have within ourselves, this thing that Jung called the Shadow.

And some call Mr Hyde.

Daimōn on the other hand is actually a much older Greek form of daemon, it's what today we are more likely to call a guardian angel or an animal guide, a spiritual being falling somewhere between a god and a human, or as the Greeks believed, the ghost of a fallen hero – something we shall explore much more deeply in Part 3.

Throughout the book with each chapter I share my exploration into the great many different, and often difficult parts of myself, and at the end of each chapter you'll find a section titled *Transformation* where I offer an exercise or series of questions designed to help you evolve.

You're not expected to write a whole book in response to these exercises, but you will be required to go deeply into yourself. If that's not something you're ready for – stop reading now. Leave the book on the bus or the train and trust it'll find its way to whoever most needs it, there's no shame in that; it might not be the right time for you, and whilst people around you might have all sorts of ideas about just how much you need to change, only you can decide when and how to approach your own evolution.

However, if you want to press on, then the skill I want to encourage you to develop is how to turn your wounds into strengths. Easily said, not so easily done perhaps, it requires a positive and curious attitude to be able to transmute violence into assertiveness, obsessive behaviour into focus and commitment, codependence into love, addiction into dedication, childishness into creativity, shame into integrity.

Personal growth can be exhausting, sometimes addictive, and often disheartening; like Prometheus chained to a rock we seem to revisit the same painful experiences over and over, usually because we are not ready to go into the core of the labyrinth to defeat our own Minotaurs.

There are times for growth, and there are times for stillness and reflection, only you can decide, but know this – for some reason, you chose this book now.

Or maybe it chose you.

If you decide now *is* the time, take a deep breath, grab a journal, and maybe even engage a good therapist or mentor if you haven't already, and whatever you do...

Don't look back.

Step over the threshold in the knowledge that this way – lies freedom.

Now whilst it's a good idea to spend some time journaling your responses to each exercise, they are not meant to be answered like a test, in fact they *mustn't* be answered because that suggests completion and, as Osho said, *where there is certainty there is no growth*. They are meant to be *lived* with. Make them part of your ongoing inner enquiry, the lenses through which you look at yourself and the world around you. Always. They are the fruits of what I've learned in 25 years of working with people and all that they bring into the treatment room – sexual abuse, violence, bullying, grief, addiction, death... These exercises are not always easy or nice, but they *will* help you to know, and therefore gain control over your own *demons* and transform them into *daimōns*.

It's not a conventional approach nor is it a formula for there is no such thing. As King Arthur's knights understood in the Grail myth, they had to cut their own path through the dark forest, for to take an existing path is to follow that of another and each of us has to find our own.

It's just *my* path seems to have involved a whole load of sex... Drugs...

And rock and roll.

Sex

There's nothing quaint or romantic about paedophilia.
The Lonely Planet Guide to Morocco

Chapter 1

A dark cloud hangs over Tangier, heavy and dense it blots out the sun, crows funnelling upward make a dry husking sound as their wings cut the air blue black against the sallow sky doing nothing to enhance my grey canvas mind.

No one else can see this shapeless mass.

Not Truc-Mai, she darts and sings delighting in the colours and sounds, the ancient walled town, her laughter spares us my black mood, this force field of gloom that arrives like daydreams of the dead each midsummer.

Tangier, Tanger, *Tangiers*... most people don't even know where it is, no direct flights from Britain which at least spares us the socks, sandals and lobster tans, the deep-fried bingo wings and salt patches beneath the distended man breasts of England that spread like a lager-fuelled contagion across the earth each August.

April may well be the cruellest month – but August is surely the ugliest.

That first night we dined at the El Minzah, all jaded finery and suicidal waiters, a below par tagine and a lukewarm gin and tonic, the ghost of Brian Jones hovering dispassionately overhead, falling into a wood-framed bed, exhaustion taking me as soon as my head hit the pillow, dogs howl like wolves and street sounds from the medina drift into a tormented slumber twisted and without relief.

The call to prayer roused me like a dirt-bike long before dawn, Truc-Mai murmuring incomprehensibly beside me, the words escaping momentarily, she slept on tangled in a broken dream naked in my arms, a fat lazy sun pulling itself above the faded apathetic mist that hangs heavy as kif over Tangier, *arrête* she mumbled without conviction as I kissed her softly on the neck.

Tu est un homme terrible.

Mid-morning, Cafe Baba, mint tea and hashish done pale green and sweet, light golden and fluffy, The Stones, Ginsberg and Kerouac on the walls, we drift through the umbilical passageways settling inevitably in the Petit Socco, more mint tea and juice d'orange in this living theatre with its cast of 1000s.

In the medina, I feel safe; its walls hold me, the ancient way of life, the absence of automobiles or mobile phones – everyone here on a level. Outside the old town energy changes dramatically, a few steps through an arched gateway the unreal world dominates once more, traffic competing with people, an unfair battle that people were always destined to lose, a hierarchy of power and automated supremacy as we vie for space in the jostling throng, back-footed, anxious and on guard.

All imbalances of power lead to abuse and destruction.

If London is aggressive, Paris aloof, and New York, for all its freedom of expression, is downright deranged, the medina in Tangier despite its sleazy reputation has a buzz rarely found in the big free metropolises of the decaying West, the ever-present hum of humanity interweaving, community pulsating as cells in a body, they pass, they smile, they glance, hooded characters unchanged in 2000 years.

As well as The Stones and the Beats, The Beatles were here once, so too Morrison and Hendrix – but they're here no longer and as is so often the case, I have the feeling I've arrived too late.

The party's over.

I look around vainly searching for a glimpse of Brion Gysin, Jack Kerouac, Paul Bowles or Allen Ginsberg but the only ghosts are those of myself, a lifetime ago darkly possessed and much younger too, my daughters – one in arms, the other running free on chubby legs, the image quickly lost as tears press to follow.

On the hard wooden seat I feel William Burroughs' bony ass pushing back against mine and truth be told all that is left of the Beat Generation is an evil djinn, broad winged and foul of breath, the self-same Ugly Spirit that once possessed Old Bull Lee, it stalks this square, typewriter ink blue as veins staining its bony, extended fingers, pale jism glistening on brittle mummified skin stretched taut over the white, eyeless skull, poppy sweat sour as goat cheese breath beneath a fine muslin gauze that separates our two worlds; you can tell this hungry ghost is here still if only from the charity shop aroma of stale suit jackets, rose water and decay.

Noel Coward described Tangier as *a sunny place for shady people*. From the high terrace of my Airbnb I look out across the brothels of the Petit Socco to the harbour, I see Phoenician ships sailing into these same waters, ancient people disembarking on the beach where jet skis now race and dope dealers ply their trade, the hard concrete floor 100 feet below me beckoning seductively, and for a terrifyingly delicious moment I feel the impulse to launch myself into space, not because I want to die, but because how can one *really* express the experience of being sexually abused; it needs a grand, tragic gesture – mere words aren't enough.

Transformation

How has your mother's spirit possessed you?
How does she live inside your head?
Her attitudes, her behaviours, the ways she treated you as a
    child – was she loving and kind? Invasive or shaming?
Make a short list of her failings.
Make a short list of her strengths.
Notice where these qualities reside in your behaviours and
    attitudes.
What do you need to contain?
What do you wish to retain?

Chapter 2

If you want to be healthy, contented, good in yourself, 'sorted', the most sure-fire way is to work on your sexuality. A truly evolved person – that rarest of creatures – needs to have gone into their deepest, most intimate, private realms and made peace with whatever foul angels or beatific demons they found within.

But what happens when the society you live in equates sex, the most powerful, creative, intimate act in the universe, with The Devil, the most evil, malevolent force within the universe?

You get a lot of very messed up, unhappy people.

For millennia now sex has been presented to us as shameful, disgusting, wrong, perverse, immoral, depraved, sinful and in more extreme cases punishable by death or worse still, eternal consignment to the fiery pit.

With such bad press you'd think people would have gone off the mucky subject by now, but no, if anything we are more sexually obsessed than ever.

How can this be explained?

It's simple – we love it.

And dig this – rather than sex being associated with The Devil, I would say that sex is God. Not *associated* with God. *Is* God. The creator. This invisible presence responsible for all life. Sex is creative energy in its most condensed form; the life force from which a couple can bring forth another human – in their own image.

Sadly, sex has been reduced down to a shameful, secretive, smutty act that happens behind closed doors, an act so unspeakably depraved that your parents probably never really explained it to you, certainly never told you how much fun they had *making* you. Sex is so much more than procreation or a matrimonial duty to be performed every Sunday night whilst thinking of England.

Sex – is art.

Sex is the energy you connect with when you create…

Anything.

Sex is real magic; forget Harry Potter, it's that invisible, alchemical spark that brings light out of darkness, form out of formlessness, and it's not just for making babies or for getting into people's pants, you can use your sexual energy for *anything*, no matter how seemingly mundane.

Like making a cup of tea. Depending on how you do it. Sure, you can smash a tea bag in a styrofoam cup with some powdered milk, if that's your *thang*.

Or…

You can take a fine bone china teapot, warm it and then add your choice of loose leaf tea (bags are Satan's testicles), add FRESHLY boiled water, swaddle the pot in a fine linen cloth or cosy for five minutes and *no less* before pouring into a *porcelain* cup and saucer. If using milk, it's absolutely *essential* that it be added *before* the tea. Sugar must *never* be used.

That – is sex.

Great sex is an art, it's about freedom, it's about reverence and it's about respect. It's rarely hurried, never stolen, and never, *ever* engaged in without consent. Sex is communication, not silence or misunderstanding – it's *interaction*.

Great sex is ritual, it's ceremony, it's honour, telepathy, grace, dignity, abandon, surrender, precision, dedication, commitment and passion.

And if that's The Devil's doing – sign me up for the Church of Satan *right* now.

The Devil of course didn't start out as the horned, bearded, cloven-hoofed malevolent being responsible for all evil and wrongdoing that we know these days.

Before he was demonised, he was a daimōn.

Pan was one of the first horny goat gods – a deity associated with the wild, of nature, of mountains, fields, groves, wooded glens, fertility, the season of spring, music and most of all – sex.

From Pan we get the word com*pan*ion, a quality I would suggest is the most essential component in a healthy therapist-client relationship – a good therapist is someone who walks by your side into the scary forest of your unconscious rather than leading the way.

To be led is to be a sheep and therefore astray, even though there is great *appeal* to being led – it means that you don't have to take responsibility, you don't have to think too deeply or even be all that conscious, which let's face it is hard work and can often be scary.

Of course, Pan also gave us the words pandemic (back in vogue at the time of writing), pandemonium and *panic*, this notion of overwhelming loss of control, the complete opposite of order, containment and tidiness so prized in Christian culture, which makes it even more ironic that we seemed to be so committed to hurtling blindly towards the abyss – the cost of unconsciousness in the extreme.

And this is the value of these old, demonised gods – they didn't require us to fall into the deep sleep of the enslaved, they inspired us to *greatness* through their deeds.

Take Dionysus, who in some myths was Pan's father, the proto rock god of the grape-harvest, winemaking and wine, of fertility, ritual madness, religious ecstasy, give me him over the Pope any day; the spirit of Dionysus shows us that *really* great sex is to surf the waves of the sacred and profane in all its abandon – *this* is the art we have lost. The Christian church saw to that, they turned Pan into The Devil and in so doing dampened not just his lusty energy but also that of the masses, using shame to control and manipulate, because how else best to dominate and exploit the mob? If you want to create *order* the last thing you need is your populace dancing and copulating in wine-driven fertility rites, it's downright *antisocial* goddamn it.

Ah – but what if we made sex…

A sin?

Punishable by eternal damnation.

That might do it.

That might keep the buggers in their place.

But no – I say fuck that, sex is your divine birthright, it's the very essence of your *divinity*, but sadly, tragically, unless you have been very fortunate and/or raised in seclusion far away from the malignant reaches of most organised religion it has almost certainly been stolen from you, and if you want to live a neurosis-free, authentic life, you're going to have to take it back.

But be warned – you're going to be up against thousands of years...

Of bullshit.

Transformation

How has your father's spirit possessed you?

His attitudes, behaviours, the way he treated you as a child –
was he tender and gentle? Aggressive or absent?

Make a short list of his failings.

Make a short list of his strengths.

Notice where these qualities reside in your behaviours and
attitudes.

What do you need to contain?

What do you wish to retain?

Chapter 3

We flew to Tangier from Paris-Beauvais Airport, a small backwater runway where Hitler addressed his troops after the fall of France. I'd taken the train from St Pancras where a glimpse of red lace as a woman crossed her legs demanded my attention – I didn't want to look, I had no choice. It doesn't matter if a woman is 150 years old, if a man gets a chance to look up her skirt...

He will.

But then – there's always something darkly *sexual* about August for me, as if the month holds the shaking ghost of one such summer many years ago, the heat, the light, the still midsummer air, the memory of her lumbering crocodile physique as she manoeuvred herself on to my naked, trembling, terrified young body, her tongue flicking out to draw a glistening wet stripe across my chest... *this is every young man's dream*, she hissed as my body recoiled.

I should have seen it coming.

Climbing the slope I could see the glint of sun on water in the distance, the warm air infused with the scent of wild flowers and seawater. I paused to pick some blackberries, the juice staining my fingers as I recalled how only this time last year I'd gathered the same fruit to take home to my grandmother to make a pie.

Down the hill the grownups were drinking in the garden and I wondered how long it would be before they noticed my absence. I liked her, she was attentive and made me feel special, but I was shy and didn't know how to make small talk and her two friends seemed amused by my presence in a way I didn't understand.

Ah there you are, her lips were stained the same purple colour as my fingers. *We thought maybe you'd run off home.*

I smiled. Where was home? I didn't know, not since I'd slammed the door of my parents' house the week before and fled to the sanctuary of her Notting Hill flat. I knew her kids from school, they were away but I didn't know where else to turn, she'd always seemed nice and hugged me which other adults didn't. She said I could stay if I cleaned the house and cooked, and now she'd fancied a weekend in the country so I had no choice other than to go on a tour of her alcoholic friends in Gloucestershire.

Do you smoke pot? Andy asked. He was middle-aged with the complexion of a sun-blushed tomato and eyeballs like crazy paving.

Of course he does, Sheila smelled of *Lily of the Valley* and gin. *All teenagers do.*

No, no I don't, I felt myself redden.

Sheila and Andy were thinking of heading back to London. You can catch a ride back with them, or – you can stay here. She paused to light a cigarette.

With me.

I couldn't think of many things I'd rather do less than spend two hours in a car with Andy and Sheila.

I'll stay.

The night air was overripe, corrupt, the sky cut by the occasional scrap of burning stardust, the old house labouring in the heat, I lay on my bed sucking the life out of a Marlboro. It was past midnight but no part of me was ready to sleep, the atmosphere electric like before a storm.

You still awake? Her voice floated heavy as the night from the room next door.

Yes.

You can come through if you like.

Okay. I slipped on my jeans and padded through to her room. *Hi.*

Hot isn't it.

She lay coiled beneath the thin sheet, the static air dense with cigarettes and *Chanel No 5*; a candle throwing spastic shapes against the uneven, sagging walls.

Couldn't sleep?

No... I cleared my throat.

Cigarette?

She never asked if I smoked before – her voice was low and husky, almost masculine.

Oh... um, yeah, thanks.

I wondered if you'd stay, she smiled. *I thought you might go back to London.*

No, I like it here, I like being with you.

I like it too, her heavy-lidded eyes gleamed like wet stones in the candlelight. *I shouldn't be encouraging you to smoke.*

It's okay.

What would your parents think, you laying on my bed smoking?

I... I don't think they'd... my voice trailed off.

You know, she shifted her bulk. *The natural thing now would be for you to take your clothes off and get into bed with me...*

It was as if someone had jump-started my heart, it quadrupled in speed at the sudden jolt of adrenalin and my entire body began to shake from head to toe.

Would you like that?

Ummm... I don't know...

Yes you do. I'm offering to make love to you.

I don't think... I mean, I'd maybe not...

Kiss me. Try it. You might enjoy it.

It was difficult, I was shaking so much my teeth were chattering, it felt surreal putting my lips against hers. I didn't want to say yes but I didn't want to say no, my brain couldn't *really* compute what was happening. I pushed my mouth against hers, wondering if I was doing it right, I'd only kissed two girls before...

Here, she said. *Let me help you,* she pulled my jeans down and pushed me back on to the bed naked.

You're shaking.

I… I can't help it, I said. *I'm sorry, I think I'm…*

If you don't want this… she began. *I just thought…*

No, it's just… I didn't know what to say. I loved her attention, it was amazing to even be noticed and I didn't want to disappoint her, it was just…

Would you like me to make love to you?

No, I said. *No – I don't want that… it's not that I…*

Don't you find me desirable? I find you very beautiful. You know, you're really quite lucky, in some cultures this is how they do it, an older woman initiates a young man into the art of lovemaking. You are over 16 aren't you?

I just turned 17. It's not that I don't like you, it's… I just – don't want to.

Well that's difficult because – I'm aroused now, she slipped her chemise from her shoulders.

And so it began.

Transformation

Were your parents physically and/or verbally affectionate
when you were growing up?
How are you now with physical or verbal displays of
affection?
What do you need to do to be physically and emotionally
closer to your loved ones?
Choose one thing and practise it daily.

Chapter 4

Original sin and the story of Adam and Eve's expulsion from the Garden of Eden – one of the most misogynistic tales ever told – began to emerge about 8 to 10,000 years ago in Persia. It's no coincidence this story appeared around the same time as the agricultural revolution, or perhaps as it might be more accurately known – the greatest fuckup in human history.

For most of our existence, like 2 million *years* of our existence, Homo sapiens lived communally, in small, egalitarian nomadic tribes, numbering no more than one million in total, worldwide. Then around 10,000 years ago some lazy ass motherfucker went and screwed up the whole system when he, and let's face it, it was almost certainly a *he*, said – *y'know what? I'm bored of running around trying to catch shit that either wants to eat me or runs faster; can't we just grow some stuff and chill?* Ever since then we have been 'free' to live separately; no longer dependent on a tribe we have nice apartments and houses rather than mud huts and tipis, with central heating and air conditioning and lots... and lots...

Of locks.

And behind locked doors all sorts of awfulness can go down – paedophilia, domestic violence, addiction, abusive pornography, adultery...

Secret things, dark things, shameful things.

And when people feel ashamed, they find ways to soothe their pain, usually even *darker*, secret things – and so the cycle continues.

Alcohol has long been readily available, sex and drugs never more so, but one of the most widespread and potentially toxic threats to our society is pornography.

And no, I haven't suddenly gone all sanctimonious and prudish on you, but I do feel I dodged a bullet being born in the pre-Internet days of porn. For my 1960s generation smut, or 'bog mags' as they were commonly known, were mostly to be found in ragged, damp scraps beneath the hedgerows of England or in the back of our fathers' cupboards and sheds. I didn't even know hardcore pornography was a thing until I was in my mid 20s when a friend brought a VHS copy of *Debbie Does Dallas* around to my place. I remember watching it as the realisation dawned on me – *my god; they're actually doing it for real.* Up until then my only experience of filmed porn had involved being thrown out of a sex cinema in London's Soho for wearing fake, bulging eyeballs made out of a table tennis ball as we sat giggling amongst the dirty old men watching olive-skinned middle-aged Italians simulating sex with dubbed groaning.

Nowadays the sight of men and women practising increasingly 'nasty' sex is no more than a click away on any smartphone. In some ways you might be forgiven for saying, *so what? Whatever turns you on or gets you off...* My problem is not with pornography per se, I haven't really worked that one out definitively, it's just not my *thing* for which I am eternally grateful otherwise no doubt I'd spend most of my time feverishly whacking off like a caged bonobo rather than writing this book. It seems to me that everyone involved, from the actors to the consumers, are all being exploited by the pornographers who are the only ones really benefitting.

We are a fragile species, we learned over millennia to be hypervigilant to spot and avoid predators, neurosis is part of our survival mechanism, but today the threat does not come in the form of a sabre tooth tiger or python; now it is more insidious, it lives in our homes and our schools and perhaps most of all in our tools of communication. When we expose young boys and girls to images of women being humiliated by men, we teach them that it's the norm, that it is an expectation, a desire to be fulfilled.

Porn isn't going away, and perhaps it shouldn't, but how we educate our children is the only way anything will ever change. For those of us already misshaped, it's harder because reprogramming and unlearning is always tough, and the shame we carry can make it difficult to communicate with our kids.

But ultimately people have *always* enjoyed and will always enjoy watching other people have sex, the problem is how it is 'educating' the generation of people born into this world of intense, extreme, unrealistic sexual imagery. Where do you go when you've seen bestiality, rape, sexual violence or just plain ludicrous and *impractical* sex by the time you are 11 years old?

I started working as a therapist about the same time as the Internet emerged, and in that time, I have seen more and more people present with the catastrophic effects of being sexually abused. A great many of these had been molested by relatives, family friends, teachers, and a smaller minority by strangers.

But then there were those who presented with the same symptoms – but no suggestion of having been physically abused.

For a while I wondered if they had successfully repressed the memories, but then I came to understand that the abuse they had experienced was not at the hands of a human – but a computer.

When these people were teenagers many of their parents had unwittingly given them pcs with Internet access, often installed in their bedrooms, in the thought that it would help with their education.

Which it did – but not in the way intended.

These kids quickly got pulled into all-night online sessions, in some cases even being groomed by strangers, but more often becoming totally addicted to the intense stimulus that happens when you mix teenage hormones with unlimited access to virtual sex.

You'd be forgiven for thinking that sexual abuse is only something that happens when an adult molests a child, but it is far more complex and far reaching than that.

A sexual abuse is what happens when anyone or any*thing* interferes with, and consequently twists or misshapes, your natural sexual development. Which means, in our sexually repressed, shame-ridden culture...

All of us.

Transformation

Make a list of your secrets.

A secret always has a sense of shame or fear attached, as opposed to privacy which is something that you have consciously chosen not to share, it's your sovereignty, it's clean.

How does it make you feel to write this list?

What would it be like if someone discovered it?

How would it be to live without having to hide these things – what do you need to change in order to transmute your secrets into privacy and integrity, free from shame or fear?

Take the list and bury it somewhere private, in the knowledge that as it rots, so will your secretive behaviours.

Chapter 5

Death and sex have always been twins, the beginning and the end, Ouroboros, the snake swallowing its own tail, the creative dance of destruction and creation...

Le petite mort.

I was young, she was old, she killed my childhood and murdered my burgeoning masculinity. She herself didn't have long to live – maybe some deeper instinct told her this, she seemed determined to suck the life-force from my teenage body, guzzling like one dying of thirst as if each fuck would steal her one more day and so by the time she was done she might perhaps live for all eternity...

She smoked too much, that was evident from the prematurely wrinkled skin, she drank heavily, I never saw her wash, she took her pleasure seated astride my beardless face, tobacco-stained teeth gnawing at my teenage cock like a dog sucking marrow from a bone.

Is it... is it meant to hurt so much?

She flares like a match to a bomb, I worry her heart will explode, *do you know how many people would swap places with you right now?*

Have you any idea how lucky you are?

So... I let her do it.

She fucks me and she fucks me and I clean house and cook and she fucks me some more.

Sometimes I get physical stimulus from it, a kind of twisted pleasure even, but mostly I'm just overwhelmed, spun-out and alone.

Predators always wait for the weak or the lame to be separated from the herd. She didn't destroy me, I came to her that way, the learning difficulties, the Ritalin, my parents, both devastated in their own ways, the neglect of boarding school – she spotted me a mile off, easy pickings.

Fresh meat.

It goes on for maybe two weeks, maybe three – on at least one occasion, I refused and slept in another room, but her rage was so intense that usually... I just let it happen.

She liked to parade me around town on her arm, proof she was still desirable, one night she brought a girlfriend to the house, they whispered conspiratorially and squeezed parts of my body like witches might prepare a stew and for a while it looked like they were both going to pounce but eventually she got drunk and decided she didn't want to share and so the other hag sulked off to the spare room.

Then one morning she announced,

I've got my period. I'm going to the shops to buy cigarettes.

Be out of my house by the time I'm back.

So, I packed the whole experience away in a box, collected my books and got on back to school... and hoped no one would ever find out.

They say all abusers have been abused.

Is it true?

I don't want to go there.

But if I am to exorcise the demon she left residing in my soul, we must.

So let's start with rape, for I'm the only man I've ever met who's been raped by a woman, which makes me think that it's not so much that *all men are potential rapists* but more that when you have someone in a vulnerable position and someone with too much power (which I grant you is infinitely more likely to be a man) then regardless of gender the vulnerable one is likely to get fucked, one way or another.

Power only works when shared, the strangest of drugs it distorts and perverts – when a person has too much, they invariably go crazy, and when they go crazy, they take other people down with them.

Hitler of course is the prime example: driven mad by power and a fine cocktail of high-grade drugs jacked straight into the femoral artery he took an entire *nation* into the abyss and ever since, like a drunk waking up from a bender, they've been asking themselves – *scheiße! How did that happen? Was that... us?*

Yup, 'fraid so, Fritz, afraid it was, but given that you are but a representative of the human race and ultimately we are all one consciousness experiencing itself subjectively, it means it was me also.

These are the dreadful questions *we must* ask ourselves – it's not okay to say, *oh I wouldn't have participated, I would have resisted* – we have to ask ourselves under what circumstances we would have joined in. If you lived in a culture where suddenly your government told you that if you didn't inform on your neighbours there would be horrific consequences for you and your family, your loved ones, your *children*... Would you have stuck by your principles?

I'd do *anything* to save my kids.

Anything.

Or what if you were a member of the Russian Army, brutalised by years of war, sweeping victorious into Berlin and part of your reward was to rape any woman you could find, endorsed by your friends and superiors – would you have said no?

If I was with all my mates and they're all saying – *come on, Jez, we've fought these bastards long and hard, we deserve a bit of fun,* would I be the one to say – *actually, guys, y'know I'm not sure I can entirely reconcile this with my inner moral compass...*

Would I?

I *hope* so, but until you're there, how can you know for certain?

These are ugly questions, but denial never helped anyone, and we've all heard the phrase *I'm not a racist – but...* too many times.

No – the most powerful, transformative word you can use is

how.

How am I a misogynist? *How* am I a racist?

How am I a rapist?

It wasn't until I accepted I *was* a potential rapist who *chose not to do it* that I was able to transmute that particular monster into the daimōn of masculinity, for the world I was born into told me all men are thus, and so for the first 40 years I decided it best not to be one at all and just shuffled around apologetically like a criminal on parole. Switched it all off. Did a pretty convincing job too if you ask my ex-wife. Didn't save me from Mrs Robinson of course but no one – apart from me – got raped.

It took The Devil to lift the curse.

Transformation

Can you recognise a sexual wound that you carry?
Who or what caused it?
How does this manifest in your sexual relationship to yourself
    and others now?
What can you do to begin to heal?

Chapter 6

Abuse victims aren't much different to war veterans – jumpy, stressed, numb, addicted to intensity, unable to deal with the vanilla tedium of peacetime, prone to alcoholism, substance abuse and suicide.

My kinda people.

I can smell it a mile off, the reek of shame, it's not a tribe you'd sign up for but once you're in it's like the Masons, there's no need for a dodgy handshake, it's in the posture, the slumped, cowed stoop that comes with the burden they carry that they are *bad* people.

But as the character Sissy said in *Shame,* the movie about the agony of sex addiction – *we're not bad people. We just come from a bad place...*

And there's more and more people who come from that place.

Now, I'm the first to admit – I'm terribly good at pointing the finger, at identifying a problem, but when it comes to solutions?

Not so great.

I mean – what *makes* a healthy sexual person, what makes a healthy sexual *society*?

I'll take a guess because that's *all* I can do – communication. A society where it was okay to talk, where people could explore and express their sexuality without fear or shame. And even as I write those words, I realise just how simple, and incredibly *hard* that is to achieve.

And yet it isn't hard, if you give people *permission*. That's the secret – we are all guilty of looking around, waiting for someone *else* to take the first jump, to make it okay. How many times have you been in that position, perhaps alcohol has been involved, someone's inhibitions are reduced, and they share something intimate and the first feeling is of relief – *wow, I'm not the only one who's ever fantasised about doing that. I'm not alone.*

But shame runs so deep in our culture, shame – and the fear of humiliation.

I saw the film *Joker* recently.

I didn't enjoy it – didn't enjoy the experience of *watching* it. It's dark, painful... sad.

Sometimes I just want to veg out to a movie, but more and more I want it to provoke or make me question.

Joker did that.

Joker is a film about humiliation. Humiliation will turn anyone dark, and whilst we can learn to tolerate physical pain, we will *never* learn how to handle humiliation.

A therapist of mine years ago showed me a statement from a Victorian parenting guide. It said – *never beat your children. They will get used to it. If you want to control them, humiliate them, preferably in public.*

The CIA understands this.

In Guantanamo, Abu Ghraib and other secret locations the bulk of torture methods employed are humiliation based – sure there's water boarding and even homicides (covered up and attributed to suicide), but a lot of the 'enhanced interrogation' techniques involve sexual and cultural shaming including urinating on the Quran, rape, sodomy, forced nudity and oral sex between these Muslim men. One man was said to have been *sodomized with a chemical light and perhaps a broomstick,* whilst another was gang raped by female interrogators.

What hurt me most, says Mohamedou Ould Slahi, held without charge in Guantanamo between 2002-2016, *was them forcing me to take part in a sexual threesome, the most degrading manner. What many don't realize is that men get hurt the same as women if they're forced to have sex.*

When you combine sex with humiliation you create a very powerful brew. It... destroys people. Sexual abuse, to my mind anyway, is one notch down from murder in terms of the *damage* that you do to another, the way you derail their lives and *impregnate* them with shame.

It's not just the more obvious acts of abuse that cause the damage. For thousands of years we have had varying forms of repression with all the consequences that come with it, and although the last century has seen sexual freedom and expression transformed in ways that 100 years ago would have seemed unthinkable, with every transition, good or bad, there are always consequences that must be encountered and dealt with.

I wouldn't wish to go back in time for one moment; I love the freedoms that I can take for granted thanks to those who went before. But with the sex-on-demand culture of dating apps and hook-up sites we have lost many of the age-old rituals of courtship and romance, so as we move forward into these new ways of relating we must proceed gently lest we leave too much behind in our haste to *close the deal...*

Transformation

Below are two lists – copy them and post them somewhere in your home where you can see them every day.

Victim Mind
Judges
Complains
Feels sorry for self
Feels like life happens to it
Feels separate
Has no clear direction
Jumps around from one thing to another
Is driven by fear
Is dramatic
Is indulgent
Feels superior or inferior

Warrior Mind
Sees clearly
Is sensitive to others
Is courageous
Is clear
Has integrity
Is respectful
Is grateful
Has an appreciation of life
Is non-judgemental
Seeks truth
Never complains or feels sorry for self
Is the architect of their own life

Chapter 7

Bou Jeloud, the God of Skins – Pan the horny goat god.

How many years ago? 1000? 2000? A goat man by the name of Bou Jeloud appeared to a musician of the Ahl Serif tribe near a village called Jajouka in the Rif Mountains of Northern Morocco. Now each year it is said he returns, bringing chaos, mayhem and *fertility*, summoned down from his mountain lair by the drums, pipes and reeds of the Master Musicians of Jajouka.

Finnish anthropologist Edward Westermarck who made several visits to Morocco in the late 19th century was the first to recognise Bou Jeloud as Pan, concluding that the Ahl Serif were still performing the Lupercalia of ancient Rome, intended to foster the sexual equilibrium of nature.

I first heard their music *that* summer in Notting Hill – found a copy of Brian Jones's recording in the *Record & Tape Exchange* and I knew somehow that one day I would have to go to those mountains, the events of that time somehow interwoven with Bou Jeloud, but it wasn't until many years had passed, late one December night when I was 40, that I stumbled across a website that described an ancient invocation to raise the goat god.

I read it aloud. Which probably wasn't wise; in fact – I *think* it explicitly said *not* to.

Okay, it *explicitly* said not to.

What'cha gonna do?

Next morning my dog was killed and very quickly things began to fall apart. I told my wife we needed to drive to Morocco. Needed to. Not fly – drive. I felt compelled to move across land and sea, to feel the change in the air, the wind, the clouds.

Arriving in Tangier in our big silver tractor, two infant children in the back, North Africa emerging out of the mist as we crossed the Straits of Gibraltar, an exquisite peak moment that for most come but a handful of times when you're just *here* unconstrained, alive, dancing... on fire.

It felt like coming home, a powerful, inevitable magnet pulling me across land and sea and it was there in an olive grove in the mountains, the smell of hashish, donkey shit and cedar in my nostrils that I awoke, the earth suddenly alive, vibrating like an earthquake, pulsating ripe, damp and fragrant as if I was standing atop Mother Nature's pubis, a pure white orgonic energy rushing up through my feet into my spine and on out of the top of my head, all neutrality burned away in one great orgasmic rush and I knew nothing could ever be the same again, no longer could I live in a twilight world of denied sexuality like some bitter monk – and if it meant I was a potential rapist?

Then so be it.

Didn't mean I had to *do it*.

I'd just have to keep the beast in its labyrinth, feed it, honour it – but not let it run wild.

Everything changed. I *needed* Pan's rapist energy to be alive and vital, I needed to be in charge of it, to be the boss, in control of my own animal, my own daimōn – in order to be a man.

And when time came to leave Morocco it took all my resolve not to point that big silver tractor south and just keep going, let Africa swallow us up, disappear into its dark, throbbing embrace where no one knew who we'd been or who we might become.

Because I knew there *was* no going back. Something that had been asleep was now stirring.

But back we went. Back to betrayal, back to divorce, back to panic, back to tragedy, mayhem, chaos, despair, destruction and shame...

Back to sex.

Of course, the thing abusers don't consider is the *lifetime* of pain, destruction and above all else shame they leave their prey to contend with – the suicides, the depression, the broken relationships, the agony, the self-enforced celibacy, the loss.

And I'd wager if you asked *her*, she would be mortified to think she'd harmed me, that there might be any consequences, and she wouldn't be unique, so many abusers convince themselves that what they do is out of love.

Because if they didn't, they'd have to ask questions they could not face, like – *how* am I a paedophile?

When you've been abused, in order to recover, eventually you have to return to sex, to reclaim the wild abandon of ferocious lovemaking; otherwise your abuser will have taken a part of you for themselves like a serial killer takes a trophy.

Like The Devil takes your soul.

They say all abusers have been abused.

Is it true?

There's a terrible truth that the minute a woman can reproduce, her relationship to the world changes, often for the worse, and like it or not I'm a part of that mechanism. These days, for a multitude of reasons, girls grow up faster than ever, and it doesn't matter how hard I try not to, I *notice* when they hoick their school skirts up higher than regulation length, their white stocking pulled to mid-thigh, six inches of exposed flesh in between...

Do I pull my car over and ask them to get in and come for a ride?

No. No, I don't.

Young girls prematurely sexualised develop earlier than ever before. That's the world we inhabit and I, in my animal masculinity, respond.

That's not a comfortable admission – but we're not here for comfort.

Is my response exaggerated by my own premature sexualisation? It would be so convenient to say yes, wouldn't it? Might make it *easier* to explain, easier to live with.

The answer is *perhaps*... but probably not that much.

I think most men, if they were brutally honest, would admit

to an *attraction* at least. Like looking up a woman's skirt – we might not feel proud of it, but we do it.

What matters is what we *do* with that attraction and I'm not going to act on my impulses. That we need our predator is without question, otherwise none of us would ever search for a mate and our species would have died out a million years ago.

But we need to recognise it, and keep it leashed.

Be the boss of *all* your demons.

A lot, but not *all* of my sexual darkness comes from being abused; cruelty, secrecy, danger and eroticism became merged – no bigger turn on for me than a vicious, spiteful, abusive, selfish and/or predatory woman. Love was to be mistrusted, and whenever encountered – avoided like the pox.

There are still dark times, usually when I'm run-down, depressed or low, when that demon stirs in me and I have that old craving to fuck someone who hates me – the adrenalin buzz of sex with the enemy and I have to be extra vigilant to catch and contain it until the moment passes.

And ultimately, I don't believe all those who have been abused go on to abuse; it's more complex than that. A truer statement is probably:

All who have been abused, struggle to accept love.

To allow someone to love you, for the abused, is to relinquish control, and when you've been raped or molested, being in control of... *everything* – is a matter of survival. But when you learn to let down those barriers and *receive* love and give love in return – you cannot abuse.

Love has a remarkably somnambulant effect on demons.

Transformation

The Power of How

Answer the following questions as fearlessly as you can, trying to remain self-compassionate and curious rather than getting bogged down in shame or self-recrimination:

How am I prejudiced? How do I objectify or 'other' people I see as different to me, maybe through race, class, gender or sexual orientation? What are the origins of these attitudes and beliefs, where did I learn them and from who?

When it comes to misogyny remember this question applies to both men and women – if as a woman you've ever wanted your man to be tougher, less sensitive, to 'man up', these are misogynistic values.

Chapter 8

Love, apparently, is all you need, a panacea to most if not all problems, but if we really want to change shit up, we need to be a bit less vague than The Beatles, we need *practical* solutions to create healthy versions of sexuality in our post-Victorian, post-sexual revolution, paedophilia and pornography-riddled society.

Therapy is probably the first step anyone might take, certainly the most obvious, but you'll be lucky if you find a shrink who really knows how to go there... you might have to shop around a bit for that one.

Then there's tantra, which took me to the edge of my comfort zone and beyond. Of course, we should distinguish between *neo* tantra and classic tantra. The latter, which I studied in India, isn't really about sex, it's more about energy work – balancing the polarities that exist within each of us, that for better or worse we have labelled masculine and feminine, in itself is a *crucial* thing for anyone to explore, and probably the best measure of what a really whole person, indeed a whole *society* can be, no room for misogyny or patriarchy in a world where those polarities are held in harmonious equilibrium.

In truth I'm not all that interested in gender – who or how or what you define yourself as is your business, although the story of an employee of a large Silicon Valley tech company who filed a complaint with HR that the restrooms had no litter boxes which violated his rights as a 'furry' and self-identifying cat stretched my capacity to embrace all differences... I guess the moral of that story is being whoever or whatever you want to be is cool – just don't be a dick about it. But I do believe each human being faces the challenge, and perhaps even the *responsibility*, to balance their own polarities. Our world has been disproportionately geared towards the masculine for at least 10,000 years now and if we are to survive as a species that needs to be addressed.

In traditional Tantra the masculine principle is represented by Shiva. He creates, protects, destroys, conceals, and his nature is revealed through the cycle of the world.

The feminine principle is the *whole* universe in the form of Shakti, her activity is to love, She is fully and eternally complete.

Shiva and Shakti are not aware of being separate, they are linked to each other as fire and heat.

Neo tantra on the other hand is more Westernised and subsequently more focused on sex, and the cynical part of me would say it is often focused on our wallets because let's face it, sex sells and the easiest way to persuade people from North London to part with their hard-earned cash is to promise them a weekend of blindfolds, incense and chocolate. The trouble with neo tantra is it's riddled with dudes sporting man buns and yoga pants pretending to be spiritual whilst using it to cop off with impressionable young, and not-so-young women. And that includes the facilitators – I know there are some good practitioners out there and good work being done, but at least two of the men I trained with and have endorsed in the past have ended up with sexual assault and rape charges being brought against them.

I for one would *never* offer tantric services to women.

That pervy little demon would run amuck, my boundaries are simply not strong or healthy enough for it to be safe for a woman or *myself* to work with such intimacy. And for people who have been abused, tantric practices can be far too overwhelming and confrontational, so if choosing that route, I would recommend proceeding *very* gently.

Then we have plant medicines, which are more on the increase in the West. Certainly, a more oblique but nevertheless extremely potent way to work with your sexuality, but again – probably not for the *noob*. We'll talk much more about these potentially healing medicines later, but the reason they can be so effective in healing our sexuality is because they offer a mainline straight into our shadow side, one of the reasons they're so fucking scary. But again, if you want to embark on a journey of true, effective healing, you're going to have to go down into the abyss at some point no matter what your approach, and sexuality work *is* shadow work – so many of our efforts to appear *nice* involve hiding our 'dirty little secrets' and unless you really have a grip on all the darkness you'll never be free sexually.

As Jung asked:

Do you want to be good?
Or whole?

Ayahuasca in particular taught me how to love, and perhaps more importantly taught me how to *be* loved. Before I encountered Her deranged wisdom all I ever really felt was fear and self-loathing, but by going to the places my ego and my mind would not permit, by traversing what was *sensible* and delving into the unknown I found self-acceptance.

Self-love *has* to be unconditional, has to be all embracing, not just what the persona will allow.

But the single most important thing you can do to heal your relationship to sex?

History lessons.

Forget tantra, pelvic floor exercises, blindfolds, incense and belly dancing, forget therapy, forget sacred lingam massage, forget 5 rhythms dancing or Shiva breath classes, forget sound healing, drum circles and more than anything – forget gong baths...

Do your history.

You are the product of *millions* of years of sexual interactions between millions of creatures who slowly but surely evolved into humans, and therein is the key to your freedom. Go back, go way, way back as far as you can into your family's sexual past, explore, delve, enquire, for you carry not only their genes but their secrets, their attitudes, their intrigues, their passions – their shame.

You are the ultimate product of all your ancestors' sexual intimacies, intrigues and infidelities, their secret perversions, peccadillos and peculiarities. And yeah, I'm sorry – I know that's hard, I mean who likes to think of their own parents having sex let alone Great-grandpa, right? But that saggy old, sepia-coloured dude was once a vital, horny young buck and how do I know that?

You.

You're *here*.

Seriously, if you want to unload whatever they have tainted and/or blessed you with, you're gonna have to come to terms with the fact that your grandparents might have fucked – a lot. And really, *really* enjoyed it. Of course, a lot of our ancestors didn't enjoy it, they endured it, but either way you carry *everything* that went before.

It won't be easy, it won't be reliable even, and there will inevitably be much speculation and detective work, but every scrap of information *helps*. Who had 18 kids? You don't get a family that size without someone being mad for it. Who got divorced, and in an era when it was far more unacceptable and unusual even? Why? Who were the illegitimate ones? There's always some. Or look at dates and do some sums, like the time when my maternal grandfather died, and I was putting his eulogy together and realised – *hold on… so my aunt was born three months after you married my nan?*

Ah…

Not the biggest deal ever but it helps paint a picture of real, sexual people, your people, who loved and lusted and yearned and everything in between. It's a complex web and you need to explore all the strands – sometimes they come together in the most random of ways.

Did something traumatic happen to your mother when she was about six months pregnant with you? The craniosacral therapist wiggled her fingers in both my ears.

I'm sorry?

Oh, pardon... she removed her fingers. *J'ai dit – did something traumatic happen to your mother when she was about six months pregnant with you?*

Oh oui, yes, my father left her for another woman.

Ah okay, yes, I can feel it. It affected the way your skull is formed. This trauma is why you have ADD, dyslexia and autism...

Whoa. Life changed in a moment.

My dad's sex addiction affected the way my *brain* was formed. It doesn't get much more profound than that.

It'll take detective work. Talk to relatives, see what comes out. My paternal aunt was a deep well of information. She told me an unlikely link to Marianne Faithfull.

1967, following their notorious bust and squashed jail term Mick Jagger and Keith Richards fled England for Morocco. Whole books have been written on that trip, Anita Pallenberg dumping Brian Jones in favour of Keith Richards en route, the homoerotic photo sessions with Cecil Beaton, grooving to the music of Jajouka, rock and roll history at its finest.

Mick's love at the time was Marianne, she who had most recently been the unnamed woman mentioned by presiding Judge Block as being *dressed only in a fur rug* to which Keith famously responded, *we are not old men, we are not concerned with your petty morals*, thus guaranteeing him a place on the top of *my* hero list and a two-year (suspended) spell in the Scrubs.

Rumours were spread that Mick was eating a *Mars Bar* out of her vagina when the police burst in. Such was the morality of the British press.

Marianne came from interesting lineage – part British, part Austro-Hungarian aristocracy, her paternal grandfather was a man called Theodore Faithfull who had served in the veterinary corps in the Great War, and afterwards was involved in running boys' woodland camps where he advocated an outdoor lifestyle and nudity as a healthy way of living.

Rebranding himself as a sexologist he wrote a series of books on the subject and set himself up in private practice. It was to him that my maternal grandmother was sent for treatment towards the end of WWII.

Along with electric shock therapy, as part of the treatment for what today would be labelled sex addiction, Faithfull insisted he must also see her children, my father and his younger sister.

He was very explicit that these sessions should take place alone and *outside* of office hours.

It was during these meetings that my aunt alleges Theodore Faithfull molested both her and, almost certainly, my father. As far back as 1927 complaints had been made against Faithfull for acts of indecency to children as young as three, but the Public Record Office, where the files pertaining to these accusations are held, has sealed them for 105 years... for reasons that no one can, or will, explain to me.

Now in her mid-70s, my aunt is still clearly traumatised by these childhood experiences, and whilst my father never went on to molest me, he was without doubt a sex addict, unable to love.

And so this strange strand connects me to Ms Faithfull, for without her grandfather neither she nor I would exist – Theodore set my father on a trajectory that ultimately brought me into this world, and I in turn was destined to become prey as soon as no one was looking and so it goes through the generations – like ripples on a dark pond.

Transformation

Close your eyes and imagine yourself as a completely fulfilled
sexual being. Take your time.
In your diary choose a date six months from now.
Now write a statement in the present tense, beginning with
the words:
This is how I am sexually...
Describe what that feels like, what kind of sex you have, how
often you have it, with whom.
This is a powerful Shamanic manifestation ritual. It has
magical qualities.
It works.
Whatever you want – write it down. Do not censor it in any
way or listen to the voice that says it's not possible.
Now make a note somewhere to reread it in six months' time.
You will be pleasantly surprised.

Chapter 9

I'm told that vertigo isn't actually the fear of heights; it's the fear of the impulse to jump. I avoid the roof, obsessing about the leap into space, the incredible violence of flesh and bone accelerating into pebble-dash concrete at speed, the impact on those who love me, the horror of what that moment would feel like – when it was too late.

I saw my hands leave the bridge, unlike the other 1600 people who've jumped from the Golden Gate Bridge, Ken Baldwin survived the fall. *I knew at that moment, that I really, really messed up. Everything could have been better; I could change things. And I was falling. I couldn't change that.*

All 29 people who survived their suicide attempts off San Francisco's Golden Gate Bridge have said they regretted their decision as soon as they jumped.

This knowledge keeps me from the roof, but the more I delve into these shadows, the more deranged I feel and the more I find myself fantasising about jumping. I cling to Truc-Mai in the night lest I steal from the bed and throw myself into space – there are moments when I feel insane, strange energies swirling around the towers and minarets threatening to spin me from my moorings, and as if that isn't bad enough...

Bou Jeloud is back in town.

The streets are unnaturally quiet, behind each door the guttural sneer of livestock as if the apocalypse has come in the night and we have woken to a world populated by sheep and goats, an alternate reality where mutton is the master race.

Planet of the Sheep.

The constant, rasping sound of long knives being sharpened on electric grinders says it's not so.

The alleyways scattered with fragrant pearls of shit, pools of piss turn to glaze in the afternoon heat as long-horned rams and defiant tree goats are dragged and pushed through the medina in preparation for the coming festival of sacrifice, Eid Al-Adha.

Eid Al-Adha – when Bou Jeloud awakes from his yearlong sleep to party, to bring madness, chaos and panic. In two days, the gutters will run with blood, severed heads blazing like candles in the streets as butchers, aprons spattered with viscera, go door to door in the name of Ibrahim to do murder with their steel blades.

There was no mention of this madness on Airbnb when I booked. We are advised to stock up on food and not venture out for at least 24 hours.

It can be dangerous, Monsieur.

My kinda holiday.

I came here to write and now I find myself on death row, confused and intrigued by the synchronicity... I thought me and Bou Jeloud had had this out 15 years ago, but it seems there is more to come.

Meanwhile the city holds its breath, waiting like a mob before the scaffold, and let's face it – nothing draws a crowd like death and sex, nothing more secretive than death and sex, nothing more exciting...

Than death and sex.

Taboo, forbidden fruit and veg, perversion, fetish, meat, bondage, Berber whores, boys and girls, girls and boys, piss clubs, leather – it's all here for the taking... we find the Hotel Muniria in a squalid back alley where Burroughs wrote the bulk of *Naked Lunch*, a soulless place devoid of life save for the sound of someone coughing up phlegm behind the shuttered windows, maybe Old Bull Lee himself, strung out on Eukodol, cooking up a batch of majoun – two pounds finely chopped kif, half pound unsalted butter, quarter pound finely chopped dates, figs and walnuts, caraway seeds, aniseed and one pound of honey.

Tony Dutch's male brothel just off the Petit Socco where Bill had a room for 50 cents a day and a boy for a dollar or less, nowadays nothing to show but a padlocked door and a lurid psychedelic paint job that does little to lift the dark spirit of the piss-stinking alley behind Café Central.

I've heard people speculate that Ginsberg and Burroughs *might* possibly have been paedophiles.

I get the strong impression that the guy was a paedophile, a fan posts in an online forum. *Of course, that is a nasty assumption on my part if it were not true, but several excerpts from both Junky and Queer graphically detail lurid, eyebrow raising encounters...*

Burroughs himself said, *anyone who wouldn't enjoy fucking a twelve-year-old Arab boy is either insane or lying.*

And Ginsberg, political activist, counter-cultural hero and America's most revered poet of the 20ᵗʰ century, was a member of the *North American Man/Boy Love Association*, which promotes abolishing the age of consent and legalising sex between adults and children.

I think we can safely put any speculation to rest.

OF COURSE THEY WERE FUCKING PAEDOPHILES.

But the speculation says something about our own denial – we cannot imagine child molesters can be anything other than horned beasts, and this is why *so* many apparently warm, kind-hearted, loving, talented, charming, *famous* people get away with raping children.

Because we can't believe they'd *do* it.

I loved Burroughs and Ginsberg, still do in many ways, their work anyway, they were inspiring, wild and brilliant... and the same is true of *her*. She showed me so much, turned me on to films and music that shaped and still shape my life, got me off Ritalin, showed me affection where there was none. Abuse is rarely black and white, but beyond the confusion what's clear is it's *always* harmful and long lasting.

Someone asked me recently what my definition of virility is.

I'd say it's being fully sexually alive and in charge of the demon, the beast, the predator, transmuting that wild energy into the daimōn of boundaried passion and vitality without allowing either to dominate or control me.

And with that recognition – the exorcism is complete.

I wake to the sneering, bleating cackle of the doomed filling the halls and passageways of the medina, and as I stumble from one unreality to another it strikes me that *this* is what we become when we are abused – meat, nothing but meat, meat to be consumed, ripe, firm and succulent ready for the butcher's steel to assuage the appetites of the feeders, powerless and without agency we are trained to follow, to provide, to nourish the gout-afflicted witches who suck our grease from their fingers so hard that their skin comes off in slimy tubes.

The killing starts at 8.30 next morning, either there is no call to prayer, or I've learned to sleep through it; instead I'm woken by the smell of burning hair wafting dirty and pungent through the shuttered windows.

Will we hear them screaming?

I don't know... Are you scared?

Oui.

We head down to the Petit Socco for breakfast, the alleyways strangely empty as if the end of days really has come, which I guess it has if you're a sheep. In the square below Café Baba boys are stoking large oil drums, roasting blackened heads and hoofed legs on long skewers of construction steel, the streets awash with watery shit, beasts no different to men when facing death, shapeless things in bloody polythene bags on doorsteps betray the murder that is going on within.

Heaps of viscera coagulate in the gutters beneath a delirious mesh of flies, dark rivulets of blood that just now pumped through a network of veins still have the sentience to navigate the herringbone patterned floor of the passageways. In the side streets hang the already headless, skinned carcasses, a family sitting together in silence morose as any whose loved one is dying within; outside the house next door a black-faced goat stands tethered – we gaze into each other's eyes for a moment as I contemplate how far we might get if I cut him free and we head for the hills but there's a mute understanding that today it's his turn as too one day it will be mine.

We breakfast at Café Central which, like the streets, is unnaturally quiet; I distract myself by imagining all the rock stars who faked their own deaths and fled to North Africa – Jim Morrison serves coffee, Elvis shines shoes, cigarette-selling rivals George Michael and John Lennon don't stand a chance against Freddie Mercury in pink tank top and jeans so tight that Allah only knows what he has stuffed down there darting distractedly around the Petit Socco in the absence of trade, *le capitain de la medina* Jimi Hendrix smiles as he brings my orange juice, Janis Joplin sashays by, a cadaver wrapped in a tablecloth like a babe in arms as blood-bloomed men prowl in pairs openly carrying long shiny blades by their sides going from door to door as slowly the bleating becomes quieter and quieter until all is strangely silent.

On the balcony of Café Fuente, a man introduces himself as Saied; a former music manager he's worked with the Master Musicians of Jajouka, now he labours in the textile sweatshops in Alicante. He's missing his wife – *a man is nothing without a woman,* he says with gravity. *Nothing...*

After, and I look for the black-faced goat as we walk back through the souk.

He's where we left him, greeting me with the same look of weary resignation, it's just – where his body was, now there's nothing but a smear of watery plasma on the brickwork, and perhaps a string or two of sinew, his head laying forlorn and apathetic by the doorstep.

It's no fun being meat, Jez; he winks at me, trying in vain to shrug his shoulders.

No fun being meat at all.

Transformation

Write down five challenging, but not impossible, behaviours
    or actions that will take you towards being a completely
    fulfilled sexual being. Number them 1-5.
Take an ordinary six-sided die.
Throw it.
If it lands on 3, do number 3 on your list. The same goes for
    the other numbers.
If it lands on 6...
Do all 5.
If it doesn't land on 6...
You might as well do all 5 anyway. What have you got to lose
    other than your fears?
Now make an action plan:

Today I am going to _____

This time next week I am going to _____

This time in 4 weeks I am going to _____

This time in 6 months I am going to _____

365 days from today I am going to _____

Put these dates in your diary, set reminders on your
phone – make it happen, change, *real* change takes massive
commitment, it's not a meme or a fridge magnet.

Drugs

I'll tell you this – the only performance that makes it, that really makes it, that makes it all the way... is the one that achieves madness.

Performance

Chapter 1

Morning, niggers!

And I'm thinking – *the fuck? Did he really just say that?* But he really *did* just say that and already I can hear one of the participants responding – *actually, I find that really offensive,* as a slow murmur of dissent begins to rise like the rumble of an approaching tsunami and I realise, shit, we've lost them already and it's only day one and all because Ian, site manager of this Nepal ayahuasca retreat, my oldest, most loved and at times most annoying friend...

Has once again – gone too far.

I'm in the bar area of the hotel, he's addressing the assembled group in the main dining room prior to walking to the remote hill where the bulk of the retreat will take place, or was *going* to take place until he royally fucked it and now I'm contemplating damage limitation but how do you pull it back from a faux pas of such horrendous magnitude and then everything starts swimming before my panic-stricken eyes and I wake with a jolt, my heart pumping double time in my chest as I struggle to remember where I am and then slowly it comes back to me...

Kathmandu.

Shit...

I'm still in Kathmandu.

But why complain? I *like* Kathmandu. I like the craziness, the mayhem, the perpetual noise, tightrope-walking monkeys, whispered offers of temple balls from the shadows and passing rickshaws, the colours, the smells, the dust, the broken-down buildings and walkways, the cries of *Namaste* and *hello what is your good name, where are you from, nice tattoos, come and see my uncle's shop...*

Transiting through Delhi I'd noticed the miles and miles of squalid brown shantytown that used to surround the old airport had been replaced by miles and miles of squalid grey shantytown, concrete for canvas, the same level of human desperation dubiously upgraded.

This is where it all started – rudely awakened from my drug-addicted stupor on the Delhi-Agra road, December 1989, 25 years old, lost and terrified, any vestiges of innocence I may have retained instantly shattered at the sight of children's corpses, fresh roadkill, pale and broken on dawn's foggy highway laying where they had been thrown from the overcrowded taxi, the head-on collision with a monster truck erasing them forever in a vulgar and garish explosion of twisted yellow steel, the shock of the accident turning me to prayer for the first time since a boy – *get me off this bus alive and I swear I'll change, I'll do something better with my life…*

A deal's a deal and so the passing of 30 years finds me grooving through the multicoloured backstreets and alleyways of Kathmandu, dust catching in my throat blended with a thousand different aromas of spices, shit, incense, diesel fumes and humanity gone wrong, cursing Nikolaus Otto who, a mere 100 years before my birth, invented the first petrol-driven internal combustion engine, and in so doing ruined… *everything.*

Sure, I'm not blind to the fact that without him I could never fly to these distant, magical lands, but fuck it – I'd walk *every* step of the way if we could return to just how beautiful this mountaintop kingdom, this *planet* must have been before the invention of cars, before the incessant beeping of motorbikes and scooters, before the soot from their engines that coats every surface with a cancerous lead blanket of poisonous silt.

Fuck you, Nikolaus Otto, fuck you for making things more powerful, makings things go faster, for maximising productivity – fuck your ego and your arrogant, unthinking ambition, you spawned a million sports car-driving wankers, a trillion boy racers, you gave birth to mechanised warfare, an unquenchable thirst for oil and in all likelihood – the death of our planet.

Success no matter *what* the cost. The true mark of a man.

This is what happens when we lose control.

10,000 years ago, the world's population was around a million people living in tribes of not much more than 150. A tribe is a unit, it functions as one, it protects and supports its population, it nurtures accountability and pride in its people, and in unison – it thrives.

But what happens when that tribe becomes legion? When it grows too big, when it bursts its banks?

Famine.

Homelessness.

Overpopulation.

Consumerism.

War.

Climate change.

Armageddon.

Extinction.

Nature will cull the species.

The only way to save our planet is through collaboration, and more than likely a fairly hefty dose of civil disobedience and social unrest. All we can hope is that the fear of extinction will bond, rather than divide us.

Transformation

How connected are you to your gut, your intuition, your
   instinct?
Think of times when you knew *exactly* what to do.
Close your eyes and tune in to this deeper part of yourself.
Meditate on it. Consciously, wilfully grow it.
Talk to it daily.

Chapter 2

All addiction is pain management.

Or perhaps we could say addiction is *poor* pain management, a self-soothing response to an inner wound that you do not have the ability to handle.

For me, transmuting the demon of addiction isn't hard at all – daimōnised it becomes my passion, my obsessive dedication to creativity, my focus, my absolute commitment to the task in hand, a furious compulsion to make gold from base metal. It's a dance I am fated to perform each day, the choice to create, or to destroy. Nourish the daimōn and the demon goes quiet, neglect it and everything goes shit-shaped – very quickly.

No middle ground.

Of course, at the heart of all addictions is the neurotransmitter dopamine, that magic little pleasure hormone that unites every alcoholic/nicotine/heroin/methamphetamine/cocaine/porn/shopping/sex/sugar/you-name-it addict. The brain releases it as a reward for eating or breeding thus encouraging the survival of the species, but it didn't come equipped with a very good *off* button, and this developmental oversight means that if we are psychologically or physically wounded we can get hooked on absolutely anything that stimulates dopamine and gives pain relief.

Western society's answer to pain has, like an overbearing parent, been to provide comfort in the form of pharmaceuticals, multiform distractions – and *stuff*. Our idea of pain management is avoidance rather than building the psychological muscle to deal with life's challenges, resulting in humans who are by and large terrified or incapable of...

Dealing with life's challenges.

Our Nepal gig is my own small attempt to counter this societal malaise.

We take people up into the hills without much more than some nylon sheeting and a few lengths of bamboo for shelter, plain dhal and rice (when they get fed at all) a hole in the ground to shit in and the hard, Himalayan ground upon which to lay their broken heads at night.

They spend four days alone in the woods without food or shelter, but not until we've dosed for three consecutive nights with the Amazonian plant medicine ayahuasca, an entheogenic brew made out of Banisteriopsis caapi vine. Used for millennia in ceremonial contexts for its visionary and healing properties, it's also known as yage, the name Burroughs and Ginsberg used during their experimentations.

The demon of drug abuse is a very different animal to the daimōn of plant medicine, although they can both fuck you up.

The key is reverence and respect.

Consciousness-altering substances are older than man and their ritualised practice goes back to our hunter-gatherer ancestors, and done right, with the appropriate level of humility, a degree of ceremony and preferably under the guidance of a shaman or holy man, they can be powerful medicines, as opposed to dirty street smack banged up with a rusty needle that's rarely brought anyone closer to enlightenment.

You see the difference.

Recreational drug use is commonplace, but it's really only in the last decade that ayahuasca has escaped from the jungle in any kind of significant way, a global phenomenon, with retreats going on every day all around the world – for better or worse.

It comes with a lot of promise, a miracle drug that some claim offers 10 years of therapy in one night, which it *does*, and which it *doesn't*, by which I mean nothing does the work *for* you. It can give you a download of wisdom and personal insight that might have taken decades to access in conventional therapy, but you still have to be evolved enough to receive that information with any kind of understanding and patient enough to process it, which in itself can take years and unless you have the right guidance can be hard to do – most of us simply don't have the references to understand what we've been shown. That kind of social infrastructure doesn't exist, partly because it's new, but mostly because it's still illegal in a great many countries. If you'd grown up in a culture where that wasn't the case and everyone you ever knew had drunk it under the benevolent guidance of a respected shaman, you'd probably have an easier ride – if you had a wobbly night you'd just pop next door and ask your nan how it was for her when she first got baked and she'd make you feel better.

The experience is unpredictable to say the least – it can be overwhelming, it can be blissful, it can be terrifying, and sometimes nothing happens at all. The person next to you may take a small cup and journey to far dimensions where their psychic wounds are operated on by higher life forms whilst you drink buckets of the foul-tasting brew and do nothing but puke all night.

You get what you need.

Some shout cultural appropriation, but even the native peoples seem to have accepted that it's out there now and go on world tours where they bring their powerful healing rituals to the gringos. Retreats exist in South America, the USA, Holland, Switzerland, Portugal, India and all sorts of exotic locations.

I took it in Norwich.

Candle-lit, walls draped in tie-dye Buddha tapestries, a carved dolphin, crystals, the silhouettes of my companions, we waited in the near dark until the brew was brought on a tray.

First in line, I gulped it down with the minimum of ceremony but for a brief prayer; returning to my bed I gasped at the acridness of the sacred soup.

Quickly it seemed my body temperature began to drop.

I was shaking, an ice-cold wind that blew from deep inside

chilling my organs, my bones, my flesh, my skin puckered into goose bumps, my teeth chattering and then the visuals began and suddenly I was rushing, hold on, I... I was *really* rushing – no warm up, no gentle incline, I was rushing like a maniac, full-on vortex surfing kaleidoscopic mandala bombardment, so strong that I gasped and opened my eyes willing it to stop but still the fractals cast a mesh over the room and I was caught like a deep sea fish in a psychedelic net with no hope of escape, electric eels darting across the walls, swirling eddies of Artex on the ceiling threatening to pull me under I closed my eyes and was lost beneath the waves.

That first night I was entertained by Cleopatra in her temple, she soothed me and made me feel loved in a way I'd never known before, dissolving a profound anxiety I'd carried since a child. The next night I felt braver, I could handle this stuff and so as I drank, I remember thinking – *bring it on, I'm ready to face whatever you throw at me.*

I vomited solidly for three hours, to the point where my ribs were bruised, and I wondered when it might be proper to ask for an ambulance...

All I felt was bleak hollow despair.

I looked in desperation for the Cleopatra but instead a vast catfish emerged bloated and glistening from the shadows.

I'm not always pretty, her mouth a wide slash across her glistening scaly face.

You know that thing I said about being ready for whatever you can throw at me? I whimpered. *I've changed my mind. Can you make it stop?*

You're a fucking tourist, she mocked. *A fraud, a fake, a lightweight, a fair-weather psychonaut...*

The swollen fish withdrew into the shadows and I was hit with sobs that burst through my body, feeling the despair and the grief of everyone I'd ever known and cared about, the people I'd hurt and those who'd hurt me, each time I vomited I felt them leaving me, a flickering movie reel of toxic waste and residual pain.

The emotion changed gear, now sobs of gratitude, tears of thanksgiving, I saw my life, my loves, my children, my home, my friends, I felt how loved I was and how much I loved, my heart bursting wide open I felt ecstatic in the knowing that this is how I have to live my life from now on, no longer closed, sullen, withdrawn and hostile...

A giant steel door slammed shut; the vault to my heart sealed behind three feet of reinforced steel, the bleak despair rushing back in as the catfish shifted her bulk.

This is not a given, her face pushing through strands of slime. *You have to earn this, what you have seen is a glimmer of what could be; now it's up to you to go out there and make it happen.*

I felt shattered. The Grail had been within my grasp, all I'd had to do was reach out and...

You've been tested tonight, she continued. *You've shown yourself worthy. The rest – is up to you.*

And so came the final ceremony, I drank once more from the bitter cup and as I did so I prayed, *please, I'll accept whatever you throw at me, but if you can find it in yourself at all in any way to go just a little bit easy on the vomiting thing I'd be forever in your debt...*

That night is mostly lost to memory. To say it was easier would be true but it's not really a word you can use with ayahuasca... like I'd passed some kind of test, my life profoundly changed forever, I'd accessed places, preverbal places, places lost in time and space that no amount of talking therapy could access, and if there is such a thing as healing – this was it.

Transformation

How well do you know your own darkness?
What would you say are your greatest flaws – are you selfish,
    mean, greedy or secretive?
Close your eyes and tune into the darkest part of yourself.
What does it look like? Does it have a name?
Don't do anything to change it, just observe it – constantly.
By simply shining a light on it, it will cease to be dark.

Chapter 3

I meet Truc-Mai at Kathmandu airport and we head to the blessed relief of the hills up vertebra-shattering roads, and fuck knows what dwells in the forests that line the slopes so dense it's hard to imagine a human has ever delved into their interior – there could be a whole parallel universe in there, entire cities populated by yeti civilisations far superior to our own, or at least intelligent enough to avoid us.

I'm not too fond of snakes, especially when I'm sleeping out beneath the stars without the protection of a tent, which is how the next 10 days will pan out.

Are there any snakes in Nagarkot?

No. No snakes in Nagarkot.

Okay cool, 'cos y'know… not too fond of snakes. So anyway – what does Nagarkot mean?

Snake town.

This… is my playground.

This is where, once a year, I become Kurtz – hiding out in the jungle, building my temple with a tribe of natives and compadres, dancing along the edge of madness like a snail on a straight razor. Forsaking denim for combats, tiger stripe camo and bandanas, combat boots and cameras strung around my neck I feel alive and masculine and vital as we prepare to face the unknown.

Ayahuasca Now.

The buses arrive Wednesday morning depositing my disparate desperate crew – tent makers, sitar players, medicine men and women, shit pit diggers, bards and minstrels, daimōns and angels weird and wonderful as any outlaw gang for indeed – in the eyes of the law – this is what we are.

Next come the punters, dragging inappropriate suitcases and well-used backpacks, 24 eager-faced wannabe ayahuascaros, fresh to the slaughter, good people who've paid good money to come from all around the world to drink this sacred brew in sight of the tallest peaks on the planet, and so it is we set off on foot through rice paddies and earthquake-shattered homesteads until, with brows sweating and lungs screaming in the rarefied air, we scale... the hill.

Our home for the next 10 days is also the local cremation ground, the hill sacred to the locals who practise Bön Po shamanism in the valley below, a religion that predates Buddhism, the sound of drumming permeating the night interspersed with screams that turn blood to ice.

We are definitely... *off grid*.

Our village quickly constructed, a kitchen, a dining tent, toilets, a makeshift yurt large enough to house 35 people appears as if by magic from a heap of bamboo poles and tarpaulins until finally, ceremonially, the fire is lit.

We are ready.

Sort of...

Of course, dosing people with ayahuasca and starving them may sound like an extreme thing to do but compared to a lot of cultures – it's relatively *lite*.

We have all of us endured the ordeal that brought us into this world, and all are guaranteed the one that will return us to oblivion.

It's the one in between, from infant to adult, that most have been denied.

When people find themselves confused and lost in life, wondering how to proceed, they've often looked to religion for guidance and therein lie a multitude of problems and abuses and rarely any real sense of certainty.

The only true god we can say for certain *exists* is Mother Nature, and just to put the record straight in case you've been struggling with which gender to ascribe to our Lord – She's a

She.

And therefore, if we look to Her for guidance, She will always have some system in place that, symbolically at least, will show us how things are meant to be done.

Take a caterpillar for example.

When it metamorphoses from a wriggly, disgusting little yellow worm into a beautiful, regal butterfly it forms a cocoon and *dissolves* – if you cut it open mid transformation, you'd find nothing inside but a protein-rich soup, a kind of butterfly sauce.

Symbolically that's what happens to the infantile ego when we are effectively guided from child state into adult, an essential life transition that benefits not just the individual but the tribe as a whole – a society without adults is a dangerous place to inhabit, because (spoiler alert) those who inherit power but cannot weald it with dignity will surely destroy the world.

Until relatively recently most societies had puberty rituals that facilitated this transition into adulthood, and most involved dissolving via a painful ordeal of some kind, which, brutal as it was, would certainly have created people who could deal with pain – and therefore were also able to experience life's pleasures to the fullest.

You can't cut one off without shutting down the other.

Women have never been able to escape pain, facing it routinely through menstruation and childbirth, and whilst men might have encountered it through disease, war or accident, these days they have little or no relationship to their pain and when you cannot manage your own pain you cannot be fully adult – you will find all sorts of addictive displacement activities and so we see a world full of frightened little lost boys in man suits, desperately hoping that no one notices that they never grew up.

Tragically the most commonly practised rite of passage these days is that of female circumcision, an operation often performed with crude instruments and no anaesthetic which can leave a woman both mutilated and without any sexual sensation for life.

The Tiv of Nigeria tribe marks a girl at the time of her first menstruation with four long, deep cuts into her abdomen, to represent her womanhood and increase her fertility.

The first time a girl of the Nootka tribe of the Vancouver Islands gets her period she is taken far out to sea and made to swim, naked, back to the shore. If she makes it, she is considered a woman.

Carib girls of the Suriname tribe are forced to hold tufts of burning cotton which cause deep injuries to their hands whilst wearing mats covered in biting, stinging ants.

The Ngoni tribe of Malawi place their daughters in solitary confinement for up to three months, sitting naked in shallow water and daubed in white flower.

Men's puberty rites have mostly died out but were no less extreme.

For example, if you wanted to become a man in Australian aboriginal culture, it required that you be fed your own foreskin as a symbolic eating of your own boyhood.

Once your beard started to grow, you'd be seated on rock while your penis was split open with a stone knife along its full length on the underside and pressed flat against the rock in order to make it *'lighter and more beautiful'*.

If you think *that's* hardcore then maybe avoid the Mandan tribe of North Dakota. Half-crazy on jimson weed, pubescent boys would fast for days before being ritually suspended on ropes attached to splints that were driven through the chest, shoulder, and back muscles.

Whilst hanging, further splints were hammered through the soft parts of the flesh.

The initiate had to endure *all* of this in *absolute* silence and was suspended until he fainted. Only once unconscious would he be lowered to the ground and revived, when he was then expected to present both little fingers on a chopping block, the amputation representing a gift to the gods. The *really* hard kids would offer two or maybe three fingers, a single digit and thumb being all you needed in life to draw back a bowstring...

The finale required him to run the gauntlet through the tribe where the villagers would roughly tear the splints from his flesh.

Only *then* could he call himself a man.

Not all puberty rites were so brutal. I heard of one where the young boy was taken to the forest and there left, blindfolded, on a tree stump for an entire night. In the morning the blindfold was removed to reveal that his father had been by his side all along, which I can only imagine would have been a profoundly bonding moment (unless of course the youth had been masturbating all night).

It's neither necessary nor appropriate to adopt rituals like those of the Mandan tribe – we couldn't even if we wanted to, we simply aren't conditioned into the kind of mindset that makes that kind of experience possible – but children do not become adults without guidance and mentorship from competent elders who can teach them to face all that life throws at us without avoidance, and if as a species we are to survive...

We're going to have to grow up...

Transformation

An old Native American is talking to his grandson.
Inside each of us a terrible battle is taking place between a dark wolf and a light wolf. The dark wolf represents all that is malevolent in our spirit, the light one – love.

Which will win the battle, Grandfather?
The one that you feed.

Which wolf are you feeding?

Chapter 4

The powdered bark of the West African root iboga is considered one of the more powerful psychedelics in the world; *they* say an iboga trip is like meeting your stern father, the medicine profoundly masculine.

They... aren't wrong.

Iboga has increasingly been recognised as a powerful aid to conquering addiction. People with full-blown morphine habits have been able to kick their dependence in a couple of days, so much so that in New Zealand it's available from your doctor. I first saw Bruce Parry take it on his BBC series *Tribe*, and knew that one day I would have to go down that road, his description of it as *'brutal'* captivated me, but it wasn't until I hit 50 that I found the courage.

With no rite of passage to endorse my transition to manhood, and no war in which to prove myself other than against my own demons, imbibing foul-tasting plant medicines became my way to test myself to the limit to see if I might be found worthy. I've been guilty of doing many extreme and dangerous things in the name of proving, and at times discrediting my manhood, but *iboga...*

Kicked my ass.

Iboga, as the say in Gabon, split my head wide open; it took me way beyond my own limits, and that's an important thing to be aware of, especially with anything mind-altering.

The day before I left for the Netherlands, I remember my 12-year-old daughter Noor questioning me about what I was going to do.

You're going to Amsterdam to take drugs, aren't you?

I don't take drugs, it's a plant medicine.

Sounds like drugs to me.

Well it isn't.

• *What about that time you smoked that little pipe last summer and your eyes went all red?*

That… was different.

I couldn't really explain to *myself* why I was doing it, let alone a pin-sharp streetwise 12-year-old…

The house was small, set back from the edge of one of those beautiful yet foreboding northern European pine forests that escaped POWs run through chased by Alsatians and men in coal-scuttle helmets, the sun low in the waxy sky making the warm glow of the shelter that much more appealing. Celine, a serene woman of Bengali ancestry with deep brown eyes that told of a multitude of psychonautical adventures, took my hand and drew me inside.

Incense, an open fire, a bundle of white sage, a mattress on the floor.

A bucket.

I'd been warned the bark tastes awful, like sawdust infused with battery acid and ammonia, but having taken ayahuasca I figured I'd already ingested the most disgusting thing known to man.

Turns out I hadn't.

At the first swallow my chest convulsed in a dry heave but having eaten nothing for over 24 hours I managed to keep the dry powder down, swallowing repeatedly to try and clear the intense bitterness from my palate.

I lay on the mattress and waited.

It was dark outside now, the room lit by the glow of the fire; traditional Bwiti music played quietly *to irritate* explained Celine. I closed my eyes and began to shake as my body temperature plummeted.

The music didn't disappoint.

In what seemed like no time at all she was by my side with another heaped spoon.

"Jerry. It is time for more medicine."

Over the next hour I felt nausea rising steadily as I entered into an inner debate as to whether it would be better to purge or hold it down. I have what can only be described as a princess stomach, a weakness that over the years has probably saved my life from self-induced debauchery, preventing me from getting as poisoned as I would have liked.

As Celine approached with the third spoonful, I was just able to mutter that I was feeling nauseous and then I was vomiting painfully into the bucket. I expected her to back off with the spoon but as soon as I paused, she was straight back at me with, *"Jerry. Time for more medicine."*

All I could do was ignore every part of my being which was crying out the tried and tested mantra, *"Dear god – please make it stop…"*

I'd been told that under the influence of iboga people often have encounters with tribal elders who might impart incredible wisdom, and suddenly I found myself tumbling through infinite time and space, weightless and without form until I crashed in an explosion of plasterboard and dust through the ceiling of a house in Harlesden in North West London.

In 1978.

Three or four old black dudes dressed in beige, zip-up cardigans and tank tops were looking at me with a kind of *'what the fuck are you doing in our living room'* kind of gaze, but before I could engage them in any kind of mystical intercourse they vanished, and a serious and powerful voice spoke in the void:

Why – are you here?

Ah, I er…

It immediately silenced me.

You are here… so that you can tell people that you did iboga. That is NOT the correct intention; this is NOT something to boast about.

STOP doing shit like taking iboga to prove to people that you are worthy.

This is not… what makes a man.

A real man does not need to prove himself by slaying dragons, scaling mountains or fighting wars. A real man has honour, self-respect, and above ALL else...

Integrity.

He follows a code that he alone has written; he defines his own code of conduct and follows it fastidiously.

And whilst this may sound simple, ask yourself how many men do you know who have achieved this?

With this I knew my iboga experience was over, there would be no ancestral or extraterrestrial visitations, no childhood flashbacks, no time travel, no past life experiences or conversations with the dead. Iboga had given me what I needed; all that remained was to continue turning my stomach inside out for another 24 hours.

I was neither awake nor sleeping during this time, I inhabited a strange in-between world of nothingness, no thoughts, no emotions, when I closed my eyes waking dreams of the most mundane, pedestrian and meaningless nature came and went without fanfare or intrigue, the only one I recall involved me emptying the trash.

Extract from that whatever metaphoric value you can.

Waiting for my train next day strung out and broken I got trapped in the waiting room, bumping up against the glass wall like a confused fly; eventually I realised the door was wide open just a foot to my left. The woman behind the counter smiled – maybe she was used to strangers arriving here and then days later leaving without the basic motor skills of door negotiation.

I left with a feeling of failure, confused and wondering what it had all been about, but for the next six months the iboga god stayed with me, his voice anyway, clear and audible giving me instructions and advice – was kind of freaky at first, but after a while I got used to him like you get used to a new flatmate.

Living in your head.

Transformation

Write your code.
Your own personal, unique 10 commandments.
Follow them.
Fastidiously.

Chapter 5

When I was young drugs were the love of my life – they relaxed me when I was scared, made me feel special and gave me membership to a tribe of my own.

I'm not the first to make that statement, but anyone who's had that kind of romance will understand what I'm saying. Throughout the 70s that was the threat from the grown-ups – *if you're not careful, you'll end up…*

On drugs.

Being on drugs quickly became an ambition. I mean, it just sounded so alluring. These people who pointed the finger with a cigarette in one hand and a gin and tonic in another were so dull, so beige – so obviously *miserable*, why should we trust them, and clearly if they were so scared of these mysterious substances, and the people who took them, long-haired, colourful people with exotic clothes and wild music, there must be something there worth exploring?

As a teenager drugs offered a ticket to the hippest, most exclusive and creative club in the world, a mysterious underground scene and an escape from the mundane world of 1980s suburban middle class, vanilla existence.

And despite the campaigns to *just say no* (like we were gonna trust Nancy fucking *Reagan*) and laughable adverts that showed us our *brains on drugs*, we went out there and broke on through. Because the fact is, whilst prohibition and ignorance means drugs can and often do kill, they can also be (a lot of) fun, they can massively expand your consciousness and they can change the world – as LSD showed in the 60s in harnessing the anti-Vietnam war and anti-nuclear arms movements; ecstasy in the 90s (which more or less single-handedly eradicated football hooliganism in the UK); and the more recent explosion of sacred plant medicines.

And miracle of miracles – attitudes towards consciousness-altering substances are slowly relaxing as common sense prevails and people accept that the war against drugs – born mostly out of racism – was always doomed to failure.

In countries like Portugal and Switzerland where they've recognised that addiction is a *disease* rather than a criminal act, they've taken the incredible step of decriminalising and even providing drugs to addicts and as a result the death toll and crime rate have *plummeted*.

That's not opinion.

That's *data*.

Around the globe different countries – most notably the USA, Canada, Israel and the UK – have conducted extensive research projects into the medicinal and psychiatric benefits of substances that were banned in the hysterical backlash against their use in the 60s – psilocybin mushrooms have been seen to be highly effective against depression; MDMA against trauma; cannabis in a multitude of ways whilst Silicon Valley runs on micro-dosed LSD. Dimethyltryptamine or DMT as it's commonly known, one of the active components in ayahuasca, has the nickname 'business trip'. Legend has it that when a coder at Apple was struggling with a problem, they would have often been told to *take a business trip*. The effects of DMT, when smoked, last about 15 minutes, so ideal to fit into a busy coder's lunch hour.

If these tales are to be believed, and my sources are *very* credible, that's why you have an iPhone. Think about *that* next time you text someone about the dangers of drugs.

Ignorance is in many ways the most dangerous aspect of narcotics, as are impure street drugs, cartels and the prohibitive laws that create and support their business and the shady involvement in the trade by government agencies like the CIA.

Secretive use and the reluctance to therefore seek medical help if something goes wrong is a huge problem and any mind-altering substance can have its risks, which is why education and instruction and the provision of safe facilities as the Swiss and Portuguese have shown is the *only* way. Deaths from alcohol are still a massive and undeniable issue, but they were never so high as during Prohibition when people would cook up their own killer brews. Now at least if you have a drink problem you can seek treatment without fear of prosecution.

Of course, the romance turned sour for me in my late 20s. Drugs became self-medication, the party was over, and the fun long gone. Addiction is never fun, but if I could be cured, I wouldn't take that option, the obsessive-compulsive drive that unites all addicts is too valuable, too powerful...

I don't know how I could begin to write a book without it.

Transformation

Make a list of the things your parents did (or didn't do) that
hurt you.
Now make a list of the ways you would have liked to have
been treated.
Get a photograph of yourself as a child and set it as the
wallpaper on your phone (you spend enough time on it,
might as well put it to good use), then next time you feel
scared, anxious, overexcited, needy, destructive, furious,
uncontained...
Be the parent you always needed.
Just – be *kind*.

Chapter 6

The first night of an ayahuasca retreat is always an anxious one for me, hard to know how things will go until the newbies have been dosed – what if the medicine hasn't been cooked right? What if it's a duff batch and all these people have come all this way for nothing?

Soon though, you can feel the shift. Something is stirring.

A girl dances in the firelight, someone is sobbing – or is it laughter? Not always easy to distinguish one from the other, a young man staggers out into the dark and begins howling like his life depends on it.

Because it does.

No, it's okay – this medicine is poky. Maybe... *too* poky.

And now the chaos is kicking in, Mother Ayahuasca has arrived and it's time to play.

Ian and I carry an almost lifeless corpse from the ceremonial space, his pasty waxen features illuminated by the fire, the total absence of even the most basic motor skills rendering it inconceivable that he can make it to the fetid pit that we called a toilet without assistance.

I don't think this is what my father had in mind for me when he paid for my expensive public school education, I muse as we struggle beneath the weight of the cadaver, whilst somewhere out amongst the trees a respected author and professor of international relations is frantically digging with bare, bleeding fingers through his own puke to try and uncover the demonic face he's just seen staring back at him from the mud as he screams another bellyful of bile into the hungry ground.

This we do for three nights.

Looking into the temple during the final ceremony I realise just how few people have ever or *will* ever see such a scene of complete primal, tribal abandon and I wonder if 1000 years from now some will talk of how we, the ancients, participated in such magical rites in our own desperate attempt to somehow save our species.

All we need now is the ritual slaughter of a water buffalo.

Next day the participants retreat to the woods alone. Here they will sit with neither food nor shelter save a light tarpaulin for the next four days and nights to digest whatever horrors and delights Mother Ayahuasca has bestowed upon them.

Now is time for the crew to relax, to eat by the fireside, imbibe the local herbal mixtures and unwind after the madness.

Which is when the rain starts.

Big fat drops heavy as frogs plop on to the canvas of the dining tent, soon the very idea of sprinting across the hill to the yurt seems impossible so intense is the deluge yet it must be done and so I run slipping and sliding on the wet earth to the sodden shelter, water running in angry waves across the floor, the fire hissing and spitting like a cobra as it fights for its life in the storm.

The tarps are bowing overhead, I push against one giant blister with all my weight; it splits open as a tidal wave of water washes over me in a torrent. I run gasping outside and begin to bale with furious abandon – 30, now 40 buckets of water but still the rain lashes down whilst like the sorcerer's apprentice I fight to contain the uncontainable.

This climate… is changing.

Almost as quickly as it arrives the storm blows itself out, it retreats crashing and moaning across the valley, it's had its way with us for now and lumbers towards Everest and on into Tibet as we sit steaming by the fire in pools of glistening water that reflect the dancing light, wondering if or how the participants have survived but none return which either means they are all okay or all dead, and so I crawl into my sleeping bag and tumble into a melatonin-infused darkness.

You must have strong medicine; the gods favour what you're doing.

The shaman wore a traditional Nepalese hat; adorned with necklaces of bones and bells he favoured a vicious homebrewed rice spirit called Raksi over plant medicine. The villagers here have grown accustomed to the Westerners who arrive like clockwork every Easter to set up camp on this remote hill; they are used to the drums and screams that match their own rituals even if they don't understand exactly what we are doing.

And next morning I question if I really do.

I mean, we've had storms before but never like *that* – that was big even by Nepalese standards, and what if it had kicked off while everyone was tripping? Cascading waterfalls whilst off your tits in the realm of salamanders, snakes and anacondas is… contraindicated.

No snakes in Nagarkot? I beg to differ. It's just these snakes wrap around your soul.

Early evening on the third night we gather around the fire, weary and a little stoned; my sleeping bag calls to me like a devoted lover urging me to bed. Outside the night is clear, if a little blustery, the tops of the trees rustling as the wind shakes their upper branches, the sides of the yurt breathing in and out like a sleeping dragon.

The fire reaches high up into the eaves of the tent grasping at the extra oxygen through the smoke hole in the roof and I'm just about to take off my boots when a gust blows through the temple blowing all the candles out in one breath.

Breezy out, I muse to no one in particular and now the trees begin waving like sheaves of corn, the wind picking up out of nowhere, the sides of the yurt flapping with alarming vigour until suddenly one of the guy ropes springs loose and the uppermost tarpaulin breaks free as the wind begins to tear it into strips as you might a sheet of paper.

Where's Joe? I shout, our woodsman and rigger extraordinaire, a man hewn from bone and leather who knows rope and canvas like no other. But even as I cry his name, I know the answer

– hunkered down in the corrugated iron potcheen shack in the village drinking rice beer and talking pigeon-English with the locals in his heavy Yorkshire brogue.

The rain joins in now with renewed enthusiasm, competing with the wind to tear our humble home to pieces and send it flying down the valley to Kathmandu. We run around the structure hammering stakes deeper into the ground and watching helplessly as strips of sheeting are snatched from the roof to spiral upwards into the vortex of the night. In the red glow of the fire with the howling gale and horizontal rain it's impossible not to believe we aren't on a ship far out to sea in a hurricane, the earth beneath our feet heaving and buckling as the wind threatens to pitch us into the darkness.

Build up the fire! Joe's back, somehow negotiating the climb up the hill from the village with reports of buildings being blown across the mountain like toys. *There's nothing we can do to save the yurt, let's get this fire roaring so if they come in at least they can stay warm...*

And if we are being torn apart – what of the punters, alone in the dark with nothing but a thin nylon sheet for shelter?

Do you think we should call it in, Jez? Ian's eyes are bloodshot from decades of hashish and worse.

I dunno... give it another 20 – see if it blows itself out.

But how can I be sure? This is no game, these people have endured three nights of insanely strong psychedelic medicine already which has taken them to the very brink of reason, and now the second storm of the week – what might this do to their already fragile grasp on reality, who will be left in the morning and in what state? Will we find them naked and broken, making patties of their own faeces, tears streaming through the filth on their cheeks, wild manic grins on their blood-stained lips?

All the while the storm rages on, whilst inside, I can feel my heart beating, not with fear even though a part of me knows I really should be scared, like – a *responsible* person would be scared right? But all I can feel is a life force and energy like I want to dance on the decks of this sinking ship because here we are, here and *now*, there is no time and space, all that exists is these people in this firelight, their faces stern and considered and I know that whatever happens we can *deal* with this, we can take on Mother Nature and prevail no matter how furious She is with us for raping and abusing and shitting all over Her and treating Her like a whore because our intentions are pure and even if we die it doesn't matter because right now we are *alive*.

Should we call it in, Aite?

Aite, our site manager, solid as Mike Tyson, solid as the mountains, he's lived in these hills all of his 49 years, mala beads trip through his fat fingers, his mouth shaping silent prayers to Shakti.

I think maybe yes, Mr Jerry Sir. The trees maybe they start to fall, maybe... very dangerous.

Dividing into search parties, we stagger into the howling forest, stumbling through the undergrowth, falling and cursing in the wet torchlight as we call out their names.

Are you okay? Do you want to come back in? No, okay – as long as you're sure...

One or two are done for, hyperventilating beneath collapsed shelters, frozen fingers clinging on to the nylon lest it be snatched into the night, and yet the wind is dropping, it screams howling across the valley wraithlike and unstoppable, and now the trees are still again as the rain replaces the night's soundtrack with its heavy rhythmic samba.

Back in the yurt the survivors huddle by the fireside, the smoke-hole above a raw gaping wound open to the sky through which the rain pours with relentless passion.

Is everyone accounted for?

Everyone apart from Max, Ian's smoking a roll-up, he looks defeated and grey.

Where is he?

I dunno, Jez – I looked in his shelter, it's empty, his sleeping bag's gone.

Now I feel fear.

Have you ever lost someone? Those words always haunt me, the words of an angry old woman whom I'd pushed over the line on a retreat years ago, words that remind me that when we take people beyond the edge to the place where they feel most alive, we risk all in our search for wholeness.

And now, maybe, we've ventured too far.

And so, we set out into the night once again, Aite, the kitchen boys and Truc-Mai, inappropriately dressed as ever in a bright orange designer cagoule. Cutting west we call out Max's name as we approach his last known location, but it's no use, the rain swallows up our voices as we reach where the hill drops away near vertically into wet blackness.

Max! Max!

What if he's tried to make it back to camp in the gale? There's no way he could have made it along these narrow animal tracks in the darkness and the howling wind, it's hard enough in daylight and fair weather – surely, he's fallen to his death in the ravine below?

Max! Max! Can you hear us? Max!

Hello?

A voice from the night.

Max?

Oui?

Fuck, Max, shit – are you okay?

Oui, I am fine.

You don't want to come in? You're okay?

No, I am fine, I stay here.

He's fine. Max is fine. It's okay. Max is fine.

⋅ This is how life changes in a moment. Just now Max was dead in a gully, I was going to prison in a filthy Kathmandu jail and all the world would be able to say – *See! See! We always said he was a maniac.*

But Max is fine, and the nightmare passes like the storm.

He was in a different spot, you stupid bastard.

Was he? Ian looks perplexed. *I could have sworn he was further down. Sorry, Jez, I must have mistaken someone else's shelter for his.*

Nearly gave me a heart attack, thought we'd really fucked it this time.

It's way past midnight, the ship groans and lists dangerously but we have survived, albeit with a broken mast and torn mainsail, and so I retreat to my bed in the knowledge that whatever dreams await me, nothing can compare to this night and soon all will be mythologised and packaged into tales to be told for years hence at dinner parties and gatherings, embellished, polished and exaggerated for the delectation of those too fearful to ever venture to the ledge…

Beyond the edge.

Transformation

Are you ready to become an adult? If so, what do you need to do?

Write down five challenging, but not impossible, behaviours or actions that will take you towards adulthood. Number them 1-5.

Take an ordinary six-sided die.

Throw it.

If it lands on 3, do number 3 on your list. The same goes for the other numbers.

If it lands on 6...

Do all 5.

If it doesn't land on 6...

You might as well do all 5 anyway. What have you got to lose other than your fear?

Now make an action plan:

Today I am going to _____

This time next week I am going to _____

This time in 4 weeks I am going to _____

This time in 6 months I am going to _____

365 days from today I am going to _____

Put these dates in your diary, set reminders on your phone – make it happen, there's no excuse not to – there's already way too many children in adult costumes running around grabbing pussy and having tantrums on Twitter.

Rock & Roll

This is the way the fucking world ends!
Look at this fucking shit we're in, man!
Not with a bang, but with a whimper.
And with a whimper, I'm fucking splitting, Jack.
Apocalypse Now

Chapter 1

Shepherds Bush – the last day of August, the sky cobalt blue, the light still piercing but through the car window blew the emissary of autumn and just behind it winter and the chill aftertaste of a breeze once balmy but now, like romance turned sour, much cooler. Summer, it seemed, was going through the motions now, as if to say, *come on, I've given it my best shot – what more do you want from me?*

Its heart wasn't in it.

The leaves were yet to turn but they lacked the radiant vitality of early May when as newborns they scream life in a near neon display of verdant lushness; now they hung lazily, exhausted and dull by comparison.

West London – birthplace of legends, The Rolling Stones, The Who, The Clash and The Sex Pistols all spawned here whilst venues like the Hammersmith Odeon, the Station Hotel in Richmond, Eel Pie Island in Twickenham and the Ealing Blues Club have long been recognised as the cradle of British rock music.

Right now though, any thoughts of such musical heritage were far from my mind as I found myself trapped behind a funeral cortege in Fulham, the forever clogged artery of Southwest London, of Sloane Rangers and sweaty back room pub gigs and drug deals gone bad on the North End Road, the girls posher by the mile and it seemed to me that all that had really changed in the last 35 years since I lived here was the volume of traffic. And so it was with a sense of relief I parked opposite Brompton Cemetery, walked across the road and through the Victorian gates into another world.

I'm no stranger to graveyards, they bring soothing and peaceful sanctuary from the surrounding urban insanity, but I'd never been to Brompton, and although similar in many ways to

Paris's Père Lachaise, last resting place of Jim Morrison, I wasn't here to pay my respects to some dead rock star – this time it was a different kind of hero.

At the cemetery café I paused for a while nursing a coffee and longing for a cigarette, my own on-off love affair with death that has plagued me for a lifetime. In Tibet, tobacco is believed to be a demon that possesses you. They're not wrong.

At the cemetery office I asked if they had a register.

Someone famous?

Kind of – a fairly recent burial. In the last seven years.

Have a look up here near where A.A. Gill is buried, he pointed to the northwest corner of a map on the wall. *Ask the man with the two big blue Macaws, he'll know.*

I loved A.A. Gill, the whiplash-tongued food and travel writer, a man totally unfettered by political correctness, taken all too soon by a *full English of cancer* not two years before, he who described drinking wheatgrass as akin to *a sheep sneezing cud into the back of your throat,* and to discover he was interred here was a bonus indeed.

The long avenue cut a swathe through the tumbledown memorials offering little protection from the sun that had now awoken, the occasional Portland stone slab of a war grave standing white and proud amongst the crumbling Victorian tombs. Stripping the sweatshirt from my shoulders I passed the grave of Emmeline Pankhurst, heroine of the British suffragette movement, until there, in the far corner, I spied a middle-aged man who did indeed appear to be walking…

Two enormous blue Amazonian parrots.

Rock and roll, the Devil's music appeared at least as far back as the beginning of the Great War in the 1914 Trixie Smith song, *My Man Rocks Me with One Steady Roll.*

It spawned a whole new genre of sexual double entendres, from the immortal *I'm a one-eyed cat a peepin' in the seafood store,* to *squeeze me baby, till the juice runs down my leg* and many, many more.

But rock and roll isn't just a euphemism for sex.

Rock and roll *is* sex.

All music has the capacity to unify people, but there's something about Old Nick's that gets *inside* you – the sex, the violence, the chaos, the passion, the darkness, the joy. It's pure white high octane energy better than any drug, and anyone who's ever performed, who's become consumed by its madness, who's become *one* with the band, understands that it's sexual alchemy of the most potent kind, rock and roll enlightenment – all thinking, feeling, performing, creating in unison, the ultimate human drive for completion, union and togetherness.

And when it works, when it's authentic, when it's really good – it's *better* than sex.

Almost.

Now at the risk of getting all Darwinian on your ass it seems to me that of all the reasons why there are more male rock and roll bands than female ones (and it's *not* that men are better musicians than women because they're not – check out Wrecking Crew bass player Carol Kaye or Lenny Kravitz drummer Cindy Blackman if you want proof that women totally *rock*), it's that male *gang* thing that runs so deep. A rock and roll band is an ancient thing; much more than simple male bonding it's a primal throwback to the hunting packs and war parties of our ancestors, which might go some way to explaining why bands so often break up before they reach their 30s – it's a young man's game.

In hunter-gatherer times a man older than 30 was an *elder*.

My experience of being in a band was that it was the only place I could encounter male company without the threat of vulnerability – it was intimate in terms of the close proximity of how we lived and what we shared, but like men talking about football in a pub – feelings were irrelevant and music the distraction. If I wanted *depth* from my friendships, I always found it in the company of women. And of course, as soon as the band broke up, even though we had lived together and covered 1000s of miles in the backs of vans, shared food, clothes, drugs and women, we drifted apart because we simply didn't know how to be together without the music.

It's no coincidence that rock and roll blossomed in the 1950s.

GIs returning from the war formed motorcycle clubs – the original Hell's Angels – as a way to stay connected to their former army buddies. Disenfranchised, traumatised outsiders, trained killers, the music became the soundtrack to accompany their angry, renegade lifestyle, whilst rock and rollers quickly adopted biker styling and so the two movements seamlessly merged.

But rock and roll is so much *more* than just music, it's an attitude, a way of life, a philosophy that represents many things – rebellion, freedom and of course, the outlaw lifestyle. We've always loved outlaws, we *need* outlaws because they stick it to the man on our behalf – someone's got to do it, someone's got to steal from the rich and give to the poor, someone's got to die in a hail of bullets and leave a bloody, good-looking corpse. And someone has to be courageous enough to speak the truth, to call out lies and hypocrisy and point the finger at the nakedness of the king, and it's for this reason we elevate them to the status of gods, and therein you have the biggest cult, and one of the biggest demons, of the 20th century – that of celebrity.

Now whilst we could say we have always had people of great renown, fame and celebrity is a more *modern* – and so much more desperate – phenomenon.

A century or so ago, before mass media, photography, recording technology, cinema, radio and TV (let alone the Internet) if a musician filled a concert hall or an actor performed in a local theatre, that was about as big as it got. Go back a bit further in time before William Caxton and you're really going to struggle to get in *Hello! Magazine*.

Go back *even* further, like 10,000 years (which in the scope of our species' existence is a relatively short amount of time) and you'll understand what this obsession with fame is really about.

In the 1990s British anthropologist Robin Dunbar first suggested that there is a cognitive limit, defined by the size of the human neocortex, to the number of people with whom we can maintain stable social relationships which is around 150.

'Dunbar's number', as it became known, states that when a human group exceeds 150 it has a natural tendency to subdivide, as once it goes beyond this threshold it requires more restrictive rules, laws, and enforced norms to maintain social cohesion.

Sound familiar?

But imagine if you lived in a group of 150. You were born into it, grew up surrounded by familiar faces, personally knew everyone including those elected to power and leadership, were known by everyone since birth, held accountable for your actions and were seen and celebrated and valued for your contribution to the tribe.

That...

Is *real* fame.

And that's what *anyone* who ever went on *X Factor* or *America's Got Talent* or *Big Brother* or who released a record or made a film or... wrote a book – was responding to.

A deep, mostly-forgotten primal need to be recognised and celebrated by the tribe (and therefore rewarded and protected and made safe).

At a time when loneliness is pandemic, the profound need and desire to connect and be seen is as strong now as it was for our ancestors, but for those of us who have neither tribal gatherings, celebrity nor fame we now have social media, a vacuum in space where we all can feel as if we have a voice, a platform – a following.

An opportunity to become an *influencer*.

When did *that* word arrive in the vernacular?

If you *really* want to understand human beings don't study psychology, study anthropology, or at least study anthropology *first*, it explains everything about who and how and what we are. Including rock and roll. Evolutionary changes take around 25,000 years to manifest in humans; that means we are identical in just about *every* way – save our shoes – to cavemen.

Within this prevalence of loneliness it's easy to understand why consumerism has become one of the most threatening demons of all time. We originate from people who lived with scarcity, who were accustomed to a feast and famine existence and so when they encountered abundance, grabbed what they could whilst it lasted, which usually wasn't very long. But now we inhabit a world of perpetual feasting, in the West anyway, and whilst there will always be poor people – according to Jesus anyway – it's rare that anyone in Europe or the USA starves to death anymore, now the killer is obesity. Our cave-dwelling ancestors weren't programmed with an *off* button, and we have yet to develop one, and until we do no matter how much we *get* there will never be *enough*.

Of anything.

We are *all* hungry ghosts.

With every advance there is a consequence. In many ways we actually live in the safest time in our entire history, but just because you are no longer likely to be eaten by a wild predator or the chances of you being robbed and murdered by a highwayman are considerably diminished doesn't mean we don't have the same instinctive fears as our ancestors, it's just now we need to project them out on to possible disasters to legitimise them.

But worse still is how we turn our fears in on ourselves in the form of social anxiety and negative thinking.

The Boss Demon of self-loathing.

It takes a real hero to defeat a Boss Demon and it was this knowledge that brought me, inevitably, to Brompton Cemetery.

Transformation

In Iroquois society, leaders are encouraged to remember seven generations in the past and consider seven generations in the future when making decisions that affect the people.
Wilma Pearl Mankiller – first woman elected as Chief of the Cherokee Nation

Create a family tree going back 150 years.
These are the people you come from.
These are the people you represent.
This is home.
How are you honouring them?

Chapter 2

Ordinarily the sight of a man walking birds would have engaged my curiosity, but right now my heart was in my throat and threatening to burst, so ignoring his feathered companions I asked, *Do you... excuse me – do you know where Tim Hetherington's grave is?*

Yes, he gestured to a simple wooden cross about 20 feet from where we stood. *He's there. Next to A.A. Gill – a man of pictures besides a man of words.*

Heroes and villains, daimōns and demons, all are important, they show us the mirrors to our own shadow sides, both light and shade, and here, buried in this hallowed soil, was one of mine.

Tentatively I approached the grave – well tended with a rose bush sprouting from the centre, ringed by pebbles, a brass plaque screwed to the wood bearing the most modest of inscriptions:

Timothy Hetherington
Died 20th April 2011
Aged 40 Years

It's a strange phenomenon when you meet someone for the first time and it's like you *know* each other. You hear people say things like – *have we met before?* Or even – *it's like we were together in a past life...* Psychoanalysis explains this as the projection of a part of our disowned selves.

Stranger still is when that person is dead, that grief-stricken sense of falling in love with one that you can never possibly meet. Tim Hetherington was not the first and surely won't be the last – Jim Morrison had the same impact, as did Bill Hicks, Robert Capa and Great War poet Edward Thomas, all perfectly preserved in character and spirit, an early death guaranteeing that none will ever betray.

Never meet your heroes – absolutely goddamn right, and no chance at all with this one, the point being they're not who you think they are because who they really are is *you*. This is the good news with shadow work – your greatness is hidden in those dark vaults along with the terrible cunt you also are; and for the British – perhaps more than most – to own our brilliance is positively *excruciating*.

I hadn't even heard of Tim Hetherington until the week before.

Here I Am: The Story of Tim Hetherington, War Photographer by Alan Huffman got to me in that way that life had taught me to recognise as important and now, by his grave, I sat down and wept for that which was lost and that which I might find.

Tim Hetherington, along with fellow photographer Chris Hondros, was killed on April 20, 2011 in Misrata whilst covering the Libyan conflict, targeted by Gaddafi's forces that his mother believes were deliberately aiming to eliminate journalists.

Caught in a mortar attack he was hit in the thigh by shrapnel – the King Fisher's wound – and in the ensuing chaos, bled to death on the way to a makeshift hospital. He was 40 years old and had most recently been Oscar nominated for the documentary *Restrepo* which he directed with author and filmmaker Sebastian Junger.

He was in a very macho job; Sebastian described his friend to me. *He was a war reporter, a decorated, award-winning war reporter, but he was also clearly very sensitive and vulnerable, and he wasn't macho in a toxic sense. He just came across as very caring, very concerned… and also clearly wounded by his experiences.*

This is what Tim Hetherington represents, he's my daimōn in the original Greek sense of the word – the ghost of a fallen hero, reflecting back to me a version of myself that I might *aspire* to – that's the trick – one with humility and integrity, strength and courage coupled with the innocence and curiosity of Parsifal, the 'pure fool' of Arthurian legend, neither domineering nor rude, humble, yet strong.

I don't know if I want to stay covering conflict anymore, he'd said the year before his death. *It's a very destructive thing to carry on beyond a certain age, not least because if you look at the ages by which conflict photographers get hurt it's usually as they get older because you're inured to the risks more. Y'know – I know when a story's good and I know where a story is good and where that is, is usually in the most dangerous area and I won't do any of the other stuff, I'll just go straight to where I think it should be...*

You really kinda think – man, you wanted this and now it's gone too far, you've really fucked it now, you're gonna end up dead, you know you've let everybody down and for what?

For a picture?

His grave looked as if a child had placed the flowers and pebbles that marked the edges of the plot, a small tan-coloured stone catching my eye with a deep V-shaped cut in its surface so precise that it could have been done with a tool... or shrapnel even.

Picking it up I wiped the soil from its surface, an act that struck me as bizarre in the knowledge that he had lived so much of his professional life in the dirt and filth of combat, and so I replaced it and walked away... but before I'd gone a few yards I turned back and – I must have walked away two or three more times, reluctant to leave, like if I stayed there long enough I might be infused by something of his spirit and so I put the stone in my pocket with a promise, *I'll bring this back – when I'm done.*

.

Transformation

Who are your heroes?

Make a list of their qualities.

Now rewrite the list, beginning each one with the words, *I am*. For example, if you wrote – Mahatma Gandhi was brave, inspirational and racist then write – *I* am brave, *I* am inspirational, *I* am racist.

These statements will be true. Maybe not obviously at first, maybe these qualities are latent, need nurturing to bring to the surface, but trust me – they're in you.

Now do the same with the people you most despise.

Notice which exercise you find the most challenging (and don't be surprised if it's the first one).

Chapter 3

It's strange... you can feel when a place hasn't been lived in.

Opening the door to my apartment, the mud from the graveyard still on my shoes, I could smell the emptiness, the hollowness of a sarcophagus. Everything was as I left it a month earlier, but... *something* had changed.

Maybe it was me.

My doormat, a traditional oblong bristle pad as adorns many millions of households around the world, is different only in that it has the words FUCK OFF stencilled across its surface.

You're so funny, people tell me.

I'm not joking, I say.

No really, you're so funny.

I'm... not joking.

I'm told my great-grandfather, Joe Redding, gamekeeper to Lord Carrington before the Great War, would stand at the garden gate smoking a roll-up on the lookout for visitors. When one was spotted, he'd disappear into his shed until they had left.

You've got to know who your people are if you want to understand how you came to be you.

You need to know what operating system you're running.

A brown envelope from the grey people at *Her Majesty's Revenue and Customs* sat on the mat. Ignoring this harbinger of doom I crossed the apartment – I say apartment but it looked more like a ransacked guitar shop, electrics, acoustics, banjos, mandolins, Appalachian dulcimers, amps and pedals all mixed in with a shit tonne of junk, skulls, peacock feathers, Hindu statues, Victoriana, singing bowls, prayer flags, antique furniture, rusting .303 ammunition harvested from the Somme and shelves bowing beneath the weight of books on war.

Lots and lots of books on war.

And at the far end of the room, a large red decomposing

couch upon which I flopped with a profound sense of relief.

As a child I used to point with my middle finger, mimicking my maternal grandfather Pete, who had but the one digit, the rest having been carved off as a teenage apprentice in the factories of High Wycombe, an incident so common it was known as the *furniture maker's salute.*

Nevertheless, with his one good finger and thumb he managed to make this large, deep red couch some ninety years ago and my mother, myself and my own children all slept on it as babies, Pete spent his final days on it and indeed, one of the last things he ever said to me was, *look after the couch, Jim.*

Of course I'm assuming it's still there, I haven't checked beneath the multitude of Indian throws and scraps of ill-matched fabric that adorn its rotting carcass for some time now, it may just be a heap of old horsehair, springs and dust held together by love and tears, but if there's one place in the world I feel safe, one place in the world I call home – it's on my couch.

Settling into the familiar cushions I flipped open my laptop and began writing furiously.

This is how books arrive. Daimōn mail.

Like the first hint of a virus, that kind of – I'm not *sure*, but I think I *might* be coming down with something, a slow, tickling inflammation that left me no choice but to go with it because, like the first pangs of labour, this *thing* was demanding to be born, and as with everything I've ever written, I knew it was because *I* needed to read these words, to hear these stories and learn these lessons that were now clawing their way to the surface insistent and raw.

A chill seemed to have invaded the room so I got up to close the window and blot out the sound of a police helicopter hovering overhead, which despite the fact that we have a *Costa* and a craft beer joint in Tottenham now, is still the soundtrack of the neighbourhood.

Cupcakes are the foot soldiers of gentrification someone once wrote and although things haven't gone that far, if it does happen you can guarantee there's enough insurgents in this part of town to fight back and fight back hard.

Not ready to return to writing instead I stared vacantly into the fridge, the blank, ritualistic, unfocused scanning of shelves, mostly bare save for a film canister containing several tabs of high powered blotter acid, knowing that I'd almost certainly give them to my mate Dan because it's almost 40 years since I'd regularly dropped acid, but like a child needs a comfort blanket I needed this little pot of eternal youth to make me feel like I was still... *edgy*.

On the shelf below a bottle containing 500 hits of psilocybin tincture; a jar of peppers in brine left by another friend unaware that:

a) I hate peppers.

b) I hate brine.

A solitary vegetable stock cube (*note to self – stock cubes don't need refrigerating*); several rolls of Kodak film and what had once been a lemon but was now a shapeless dollop of furry blue jelly with potentially more psychedelic properties than the LSD and mushrooms combined given my fridge had chosen to die in my absence and transform into a hot box of not inconsiderable toxicity.

Last but not least, a bag of iboga – too strong to take, too sacred to throw away, doomed to reside in my fridge in perpetuity.

I backed away, the very sight of the medicine giving me chills even though the icebox was shot, and whom was I fooling anyway, I wasn't hungry, I was just distracting from *the process*, the exploration, avoiding what I might find if I had the courage to follow Tim Hetherington down into the underworld and so I returned once more to my decrepit couch and gazed into the dark mirror of my MacBook.

Transformation

Imagine a party.

You walk into a room jam-packed with your ancestors, your people – your blood.

What does that feel like? Is it joyful or threatening? Do they turn and beam with delight as you walk in the room or does it fall silent like a wild west saloon?

Who do you feel drawn to? Who do you want to avoid?

Do you feel proud to be from this clan?

Chapter 4

Autumn crept into winter.

In Tesco's they had an offer on *Franziskaner Weissbier*, 3 for £5.25, so I put them in my trolley because I like wheat beer but then I remembered wheat beer is totally gay and so I put them back on the shelf and tried to gage what Billy and Dan might like... It took a good few minutes of walking up and down the aisle until I settled for *Duval* which I don't like but I figured they would because it's bitter and strong and more manly and I could imagine us sitting on the wet French ground with hunks of bread and cheese and drinking *Duval* like men.

The journey down to the Somme was uneventful once we'd retrieved Billy's forgotten passport from his house; ribbing each other about our musical taste I forged an evil alliance with Billy against Dan with *The Clash* because I know Billy ran with them when they were at the height of their powers, and as *I Fought the Law* showed off exactly what my sub-woofer was capable of the first of the war cemeteries appeared across the open countryside.

Truc-Mai didn't care what music we played, she didn't really understand what any of this was about, she knew nothing of war, her parents having successfully shielded her from the horrors of their native Vietnam, nevertheless she laughed with delight and excitement, breathing in the testosterone infusing the car.

Truc-Mai was born laughing.

At Vimy Ridge we paused a while as the light began to falter. A cold, bloody watercolour smear blooming above the sombre woodland, the grief-stricken monument to the Canadian dead cast a long, mournful shadow across the old battlefields, the wind whipping bitter and sharp enough to freeze us like these statues that gave little clue to what really happened here on this manicured plateau. Dan climbed the cadaverous steps shooting his camera from the hip, Billy wandered lost in thought whilst

Truc-Mai seemed confused trying to comprehend the irregular undulations of the earth like so many petrified waves where once shells tore men to scraps of wet flesh, the signs warning still *danger – unexploded ordinance*, and then we were off again into the night, the wipers screeching across my windscreen like so many nails down a blackboard, the graveyards more regular now, headstones glaring bone white in the starlit fields.

Eventually the chateau appeared out of the mist, an ancient rotting heap just behind the old front lines where once Generals poured over trench-maps devising Claret-addled strategies that doomed the youth who now sleep in these fields for all perpetuity.

They burp so much, Truc-Mai observed, both intrigued and perplexed at the way my companions expressed themselves so freely.

Did he really just fart?

And yes Billy and Dan really *did* burp and fart for they are men and men both fart and burp, what's more they ate hunks of cheese and spicy sausage with their bare hands washed down with glasses of wine and French brandy – although they seemed disinterested in the *Duval* – but the brandy was good as was the wine and so they burped and farted and drank and ate and we laughed together in the kitchen while I prepared a supper of fierce spicy dhal.

The old house was haunted, that much was clear, some parts unnaturally cold, the snooker room like a morgue, the cellar too dark to even contemplate, the SS had their headquarters here in the second war and at all times...

I felt observed.

Next morning, we rose at dawn; greeting the dying year with sore heads we drove towards a salmon flesh sunrise that struggled to penetrate the grimy wet morning, Billy complaining that Dan had kept him awake all night with a surprise gas attack.

Leaving the car beside a heap of manure we adjusted our

backpacks, fastening sleeves and collars against the cold all *Gore-Tex* and *North Face* except for Truc-Mai who, fresh from Paris, seemed not to have grasped the magnitude of this agricultural shit-fest as she donned her transparent Muji raincoat and I found myself wondering which part of *y'know it's gonna be really fucking cold don't you?* she hadn't understood, as we slipped and slid through the greasy blood and bone rich soil; it clung to our boots doubling their weight by the time we reached the thin line of barbed wire that separated us from the Newfoundland Memorial Park and suddenly I was back to where it all started – here, on this preserved killing ground, all those years ago now, driving back from a summer holiday that I was first rudely shaken from the long sleep of youth.

With every signpost that flashed by the car – *Beaumont-Hamel, Albert, Auchonvillers, Bapaume, Poziéres, Mametz, Thiepval* – the emotion brewing and tumbling and building like the swollen rumblings of a summer storm, and then the cemeteries began to appear on the horizon, in the middle of a field, by a roadside, on top of a distant hill… *everywhere.* And in the verges and beneath hedgerows heaps of unexploded shells, rusty barbed wire strung still between forgotten trenches, shrapnel and .303 clips in the furrows, and in a wood by the name of Hangard a German water canteen, rudely pierced by a bullet.

Something inside me snapped, the armour pierced.

The numbness that had kept me safe and unfeeling like a vampire's shroud gave way to raw emotion; the trauma held in that soil, the tears, the blood, the blood of men, the blood of mere boys, the suffering, the breathless, heart-stopping fear, the shock, the horror, the blood, the blood and the tears rushing like molten sadness up through the soles of my feet and into my veins, consuming me with grief, a grief I didn't even know I was carrying so complete was my deadness, a grief that was mine and a grief that was theirs, the links falling from my armour like petals from a rose.

I paused in a moment of reflection, facing the old German line and for a moment all was still save for my heart, even the birds silent, and then, gathering myself, I climbed the wire...

And followed Billy in.

Transformation

How does your family manage pain?
What is unspeakable in your family and how does that silence
   affect your relationship with yourself and with others?

Chapter 5

There's a reason that men have traditionally queued up and often lied about their age to go to war. It gives meaning and a sense of brotherhood so often absent in everyday life.

This is what brought me, time and time again, to the old battlefields, just as it had brought me to Tim Hetherington's grave, the search for my lost people, a deep and profound need for a sense of belonging, and in the Great War this natural tendency to bond in groups was exploited in a recruitment strategy that became known as the Pals Battalions. It promised young men that they would be allowed to serve with their friends if they signed up together, and people responded in their droves, the menfolk from entire football teams and villages and towns joined up with their mates and marched off to war...

Together.

Kitchener appealed for 500,000 volunteers.

He got 2.5 million.

There was just one flaw in the system that no one had considered.

Not only did they join up together, train together and embark for the front together...

They were massacred together.

The extent of the slaughter goes a long way to explaining just how deeply the Somme was felt, is *still* felt, at home. The death toll was not diluted...

It was condensed.

The Pals Battalions of July 1st 1916 made up many of the 57,470 men who fell that day, most within the first half hour, a day that constitutes the worst in British military history. There's something in the comradeship, the integrity and the willingness of Kitchener's Army to answer the call to arms and the subsequent criminal arrogance of those in power that led to the slaughter of so many that cuts deep to this day still.

And writing those words I suddenly realise I'm also talking about my father as I recall my desperate eagerness to please him be it through academia or sport, the eagerness of a boy who will do anything for the approval of a father, and how time and time again I was met with a barrage of rage and humiliation.

The eagerness to please a fatherly figure, something all boys share, was what Lord Kitchener had harnessed when he called for recruits in 1914.

Look at any war memorial and take a moment to imagine how the loss of so many, often with the same surname, affected these small rural East Lancashire towns such as Accrington, Burnley, Blackburn, and Chorley where literally hundreds of telegrams from the war office regretting the deaths of so many arrived...

All on the same day.

Of the 700 men from Accrington who went over the top in front of the village of Serre that morning, 585 men became casualties – 235 killed and 350 wounded in about half an hour. The dead lay where they fell for months and when the bones were finally collected a great many couldn't be identified.

I don't know how you get your head around that? How do we relate? Can you imagine 235 pupils from your school being wiped out in half an hour?

I've been to that spot where the Accrington Pals were murdered, the trench still remains, although much shallower now, at the edge of a small wood peppered with shell-holes and wreathes which are still left to this day, and in front... a wide-open field devoid of any cover, in the centre of which is a cemetery. That's as far as they got that day and that's where they will stay in perpetuity.

Together.

I spoke to a friend of mine, legendary Vietnam War photographer Tim Page, acid head, rock and roller and living embodiment of Robert Capa's ethos – *if your photographs aren't good enough, you're not close enough.* Badly wounded four times, declared dead more than once, the inspiration for Dennis Hopper's character in *Apocalypse Now* and brother-in-arms of Errol Flynn's son Sean, he described to me the bond that makes men at war so *tight.*

I mean – it's without doubt true that you form bonds... the bloke next to you in the trench, or in the foxhole or in the bunker is the person who's going to be there when you're wounded.

You eat... you shit... you die... you have no embarrassments when things come down to that basic level, you've gotta survive, you've gotta take a shit, you gotta lose your arm, you gotta do whatever it is... and that person, that mate, that buddy, is more than a brother, is more than a father, you become über close, there are no restrictions, there is an openness, a totally open chakra, this umbilical cord of light that joins you so you only need to say three words and you've summed up the whole fucking moment...

An umbilical cord of light. The same can perhaps be said of musicians.

I think it's a very poignant thing that after you've been on the road for like 50 plus years, Mick Jagger said after they played in Cuba for the first time in 2016, *that you can still get together and actually have a goal and achieve it.*

There is something there that sticks us together, Keith agreed. *It's nothing you'd ever catch us talking about. I feel incredibly blessed really.*

It's a sort of camaraderie isn't it, Charlie Watts said. *You don't say anything but you know what Ronnie means or what Keith's laughing at, or Mick won't even say anything... it's as deep as that I suppose.*

But the fact is it doesn't matter whether it's rock and roll or war or nature that you go up against, what matters is the sense of togetherness, it's tribal, it's about commitment to each other, it's about a common cause, it's not about selfishness, greed and apathy, it's about helping your brother when he falls...

It's about *love.*

The sad fact is that whilst our society today, on the whole, is the safest, the most materially wealthy, and the most technologically advanced of all time...

It's by *far* the loneliest.

And that's what ultimately took me to drug culture, the Somme, and a graveyard in West London – just another dispossessed soul looking for a tribe.

Transformation

Decide when you're going to die.
Pick an age that you'd like to live to and commit to it, do
  everything in your power to make it to that age and live
  your life in the belief that you'll get there.

Now imagine you have arrived at that age and you're looking
back over your life – what do you want to have accomplished?
Make a list of the things that are most important for you to
have achieved by then and do not rest until you've made
them all happen.

Chapter 6

Once over the wire we walked amongst the shell-holes and trenches – safe and sanitised now compared with my first visit a quarter of a century ago when sheep got caught on the barbed wire and unexploded shells lay scattered across the old killing ground, but still the earth holds the tears of all those that have paid homage over the years to this place where, of the 801 Newfoundlanders who went into battle, only 68 answered roll call the following day.

The rain began as we walked, mostly in silence, down past Y Ravine, scene of fierce hand-to-hand fighting at the end of the battle, and out across the fields, the occasional unexploded shell rusty and menacing in our path, the sweet smell of silage on the air, our cheeks cold in the early morning breeze that cut across the poisoned farmland and I wondered how men could live let alone *fight* here – it's one thing to imagine cheering armies marching through pastures of butterflies and poppies waving tin hats at the camera but spending a winter in this shit is beyond comprehension. I'd only been walking for half an hour and already my feet were wet and sore, my face numb from the cold.

Hunched over beneath a bruised sky we pushed into the rain, it beat against us with a new determination, and try as I might it was impossible to really comprehend what had happened here. Different battlefields have different atmospheres, different ghosts. Omaha Beach in Normandy is poignant and terrifying in just how exposed it feels. Verdun I could not get away from fast enough so dark was the energy, even the locals questioning why I would venture there – *it is the place of the dead, Monsieur.*

The Somme has an atmosphere not unlike a church, a vast outdoor cathedral infused with the emotion of all those who died here and all who subsequently came to mourn, but its stillness is unnatural and woe betide any who linger past nightfall, especially in the dark woods that locals and visitors alike claim are the realm of spectres and ghouls – how could they not be?

The clouds now so low it felt like we were carrying them on our backs as we trudged up the hill to the great lumbering obscenity that is the Thiepval Memorial, Edwin Lutyens' brutal and overwhelming edifice to the missing 72,000 men who simply vanished into the mire, their bones held captive in the very same mud that now clung to our boots, the weight of their suffering in our every step.

Heads down against the rain I snatched the occasional shrapnel ball from the roadside, residue of the iron harvest that still plagues those who try to farm this toxic soil, and by the time we got to the top Dan was finished. Lovesick, he was in no mood for the pain of this place or the weather, and I forgot the fucking *Duval* back at the chateau so I couldn't even offer him a beer to cheer him up.

Secretly, I was relieved.

My feet were wet and beginning to blister and I couldn't help thinking of men in boots far more unforgiving than mine who had to march through this land with raw and bleeding soles. But that only made me feel worse and no one seemed to mind when I suggested cutting the walk short; and so we dragged ourselves back down the valley and up the other side until my legs finally refused to go another step and so I leaned into the icy wind and rain with Truc-Mai by the roadside waiting for Dan to return with the car.

I don't even know why we're here?

Dan was genuinely confused; his first time on the Somme and I couldn't answer him... it's a compulsion I gave up trying to fully understand years ago.

Now – I just come.

Truc-Mai had long gone to bed, and so without the social

programming that tells men to be strong and silent in the presence of a woman, they began to open up.

It's a pilgrimage.

Billy's jaw was tight with emotion; he and I first came here 17 years ago, three days after 9/11.

Jesus, I'm covered in Dad, he muttered, mostly to himself, brushing his father's ashes from the inside of his walking trousers, the residue of a scattering several summers ago. *It's a pilgrimage,* he continued, *it calls me, it comes from deep within...*

Thiepval honours the missing men of the Somme, but I couldn't help wondering – what honour for the missing men of my generation? The half-dead, suicidal, listless and hollow men who amble through life in sexless marriages trudging to jobs they hate without purpose or pride in what they do or who they are?

Clearly... I was not in a positive mood.

Next day we split – Truc-Mai back to Paris, Dan, Billy and myself missing our crossing and so we sat in the Eurotunnel car park for three hours smoking cigars and drinking red wine out of paper cups, looking at the world so many had died to preserve, *Burger King, World Duty Free, WH Smith...*

Starbucks.

I stubbed the Havana out in the dregs of my wine – it had become too bitter for my palate.

When we finally got to Folkestone the car wouldn't start so Dan and Billy pushed it off the train, screaming at me to put it in second and release the clutch but... I've never jump-started a car before.

What a fucking idiot, Dan shouted in frustration, but then some real men in a tow truck came and got us started and so with my ego in tatters, we limped back on to British soil.

And that's just a fact – real men know how to jump-start cars. Dan and Billy are real men, they burp and fart and chop wood and have tools and jump-start cars and know what a carburettor looks like and how to use a chainsaw, and as usual I'm just too sensitive and feminine to ever really belong and I realised that, just like Billy's dusty dead dad in his pants, somehow my father had slipped unnoticed into the car that weekend and I was nine years old again and he was standing over me smelling of beer and tobacco and we do that war of attrition thing where he tells me just how ashamed and disgusted he is by me and I grit my teeth and set my jaw determined not to cry but I know in the end that he will win because he always does.

It was late and we broke the journey, stopping for the night at Billy's ancient shack on the beach with timbers that groan in the night and a wind that seemed to want to fling us back into the sea, and I curled in the damp bed never more grateful for the grey sleep that took me as soon as my head hit the pillow.

In the shocking morning light we walked through a post-apocalyptic landscape of shacks, rusting iron and verdigris of copper, driftwood, shells, feathers, plastic and everything the sea shits back on to the land. Past the power station and along the shingle we stop to watch the artistry with which the fishermen beach their boat and drag it up the slope away from the foam.

They're the last great hunter-gatherers, Billy seemed to be thinking aloud. *They go out at 4am no matter the weather against this sea to catch whatever's out there; they've been here forever...*

But as I gazed at their young, ruddy faces all I could see were those who left these shores long ago and now lie in neat rows across the water in the cold damp soil of France, and so I turned and walked back across the shingle to the warmth of the cabin.

Transformation

Who has died in your life?
Have you allowed yourself to grieve?
How was their death dealt with?
Can you talk openly about your loss?

Chapter 7

The single most dangerous word in the English language is *normal*.

Once upon a time it was normal to live in small tribes of nomadic hunter-gatherers who had no notion of ownership or possessions, simple people who lived a mostly egalitarian way of life with minimal impact on the environment that sustained them.

These early humans – who make up most of our history – understood the importance of pooling resources. It wasn't about being *nice*. It was about surviving. Sharing the day's hunt meant that everyone got a piece of the action, it didn't matter if you lucked out or not, whatever the outcome you were going to get *fed*.

Eventually the old ways were replaced with a new kind of normality as the invention of farming brought catastrophic consequences for humanity, the accumulation of wealth meaning women were relegated to the role of reproduction with a subsequent population explosion that necessitated cities, which in turn unleashed a legion of problems that have now become normal in modern day culture – depression, suicide, divorce, consumerism, debt, crime and industrialised warfare.

Ancient people had tribal disputes and occasional battles that usually ended when one warrior was killed or wounded and thus honour and peace restored. But over the millennia we became better and better at killing each other until during the Great War it became normal to slaughter men by the millions, just as how a generation later it became normal to kill millions more, including the mass deportation and extermination of the Jews of Europe.

Afterwards it became normal to grieve in secret, not to mention the war or the fact that grandad jumps every time a car backfires or that grandma cries every year on the same date.

But it's not just the normalisation of obvious horror that is the problem, it's the subtler, more insidious things that erode our well-being.

Divorce has become normal, and with it the single-parent family. The old proverb *it takes a village to raise a child* is so true, but the village has been replaced by day-care nurseries as parents drag their exhausted selves to work to meet the need for two incomes as basic costs of living spiral out of control whilst we stand by and watch helplessly as the nuclear family collapses.

In his amazing book *Tribe: On Homecoming and Belonging*, Sebastian Junger observes, *the alienating effects of wealth and modernity on the human experience start virtually at birth and never let up. Infants in hunter-gatherer societies are carried by their mothers as much as 90 percent of the time, which roughly corresponds to carrying rates among other primates.*

In America during the 1970s, mothers maintained skin-to-skin contact with babies as little as 16 percent of the time, which is a level that traditional societies would probably consider a form of child abuse.

Child abuse.
We have *normalised* a form of child abuse.

Also unthinkable would be the modern practice of making young children sleep by themselves, Sebastian continues. *Humans are primates – we share 98 percent of our DNA with chimpanzees – and primates almost never leave infants unattended, because they would be extremely vulnerable to predators. Infants seem to know this instinctively, so being left alone in a dark room is terrifying to them.*

I remember being alone in my room at night, a bolt on the door to keep me locked in, terrified of the ghosts who lived in my curtains; of the evil old man beneath my bed – I used to take a running jump at my cot so that his bony old hands wouldn't grab my ankles and pull me under.

What Sebastian Junger says is a shocker – the majority of us have been brought up in a way, a conventional way that on the whole everyone accepts, and yet has damaged us profoundly. We are designed to sleep with our parents whose job it is to protect us from predators.

You know that time of night when if you wake up you obsess about your tax return or losing your job or that no one likes you?

It's not just me, right?

It's around 3.30am. *'The darkest hour'*. Once again that's ancestral memory at play. 3.30am is the time when human predators – snakes, sabre tooth tigers et cetera – were most active. It's when we were at our most vulnerable. So you can put all the locks on all the doors you like, a baby that wakes in the night doesn't know there's nothing out there to eat it anymore, not in the West anyway – it's responding to instinct.

Can you imagine how terrifying that is?

Or worse still, given that it almost certainly happened to you, can you *remember* how terrifying that *was*?

And then you apply that to an entire society?

Trauma becomes normal. And then you have a species of disconnected, desensitised, selfish people who are no longer here for the tribe but are out to look after themselves, no matter what the cost, even if that cost is extinction.

As we have seen with wealth came the need for locks, with locks came possessions, with possessions came the notion of ownership, which became extended to *women*, which gave birth to...

Misogyny.

But that was okay, because to take ownership of women, to pay them less, to regard them as inferior, to deny them equal rights...

Was now normal.

And whilst misogyny is of course most commonly directed

towards women, it can be extended towards *anything* considered feminine, which includes...

Mother Nature.

And so soon it became normal to fill her oceans full of plastic, to pump her atmosphere full of poison, to tear down her forests and cover her over in concrete, to plunder her resources, until suddenly climate change became normal with the very *future* of our species hanging precariously in the balance and all those post-apocalyptic movies you watched with your hand in a box of popcorn seem to be coming true.

Of course, there's no point in romanticising – much as we might like to, no one is going back to a hunter-gatherer existence, it's too late. I mean, you *could* try approaching the Sentinelese people of the Andaman Islands, but I wouldn't advise it because they'll kill you, and quite right too, they don't need the likes of you fucking up their untouched island paradise with your Western imperialist values and pathogens. No – the *real* point is to acknowledge what we've lost, and reclaim what we can, in whatever way we can, and *this* is why we must throw ourselves on Mother Nature's altar and beg...

For forgiveness.

Transformation

What have you learned to ignore?

What have you had to do to be able to walk by the homeless person on your street, the refugee begging at the station? How do you see them? Do you see them at all?

What does it do to you to switch off?

What does it do to you to switch back on?

Chapter 8

You know, to be completely honest, I'm a bit tired of this culture of guilt tripping people for using plastic bags or owning cars or taking baths rather than showers.

It's not that we shouldn't all do our bit for the environment, we must, but the reality is that about 100 companies like ExxonMobil, Shell, BP and Chevron are responsible for 71% of greenhouse gas emissions. These are the culprits, the oil and coal industries, and no matter how much you recycle unless we campaign to our governments to bring about radical policy change in relation to these self-serving monsters...

We're all going to be toast.

And I know, I know – at times it feels overwhelming when confronted with our own sense of powerlessness as these demons rape and pillage our planet for their own gain, oblivious to the carnage and suffering that surrounds us all.

But when you're feeling powerless and despondent, all you have to do is look back over the last 100 years and remember...

Shit has *changed*, man.

If we just use the USA as a representation of societal evolution... shit has *really* changed. The 20th century was perhaps the most condensed period of turbulence and social unrest, like... *ever?* In that time we've seen women get the vote; the legalisation of contraception and abortion; Rosa Parks refusing to get to the back of the bus; in 1964, the year I was born, the Civil Rights Act formally prohibited discrimination based on race, colour or religion, and the following year the Voting Rights Act extended the vote to all races.

Of course, when it comes to racism nowhere near enough has changed. It's baffling to me that we even *need* a campaign that states Black Lives Matter. What kind of world do we live in where that even needs to be said? *Debated* even. But we *do* and it *does* because black people are routinely shot and killed at a disproportionately higher rate than white people in America, and as I write police stations are burning and tear gas fills the air of US cities and as blood congeals in sticky pools beyond the razor wire fences that surround the White House.

There is still much work to be done.

But mark my words, shit's gonna change around here, and if you're still feeling powerless and despondent, consider this – in December 1903 Orville and Wilbur Wright made the first controlled, sustained flight of a powered, heavier-than-air aircraft four miles south of Kitty Hawk, North Carolina and 66 years later on July 20, 1969, at 20:17 UTC Neil Armstrong and Buzz Aldrin landed...

On the fucking *moon*.

So if you're wondering how we're going to make these changes?

Trust. It'll happen. All you have to do is show up.

I used to be in a rock and roll band, now I run men's groups – there's a lot of similarities, it's just we don't have to wait for the drummer anymore, but we are still a band, a brotherhood with the common aim of supporting each other.

That's tribal.

So too, I live in a building that has a strong sense of community, we look out for one another and perhaps most radical of all – we smile and say hello when we pass in the corridors.

Find out who your neighbours are. They matter. They used to be the people who would *die* for you.

When you know your people and your people know *you*, not only will you feel happier, but you'll be safer too. People don't hurt other people. People hurt bitches, assholes, dickheads, cunts and motherfuckers, people hurt niggers, pakis, chinks and wogs, just like soldiers kill gooks, bad guys, krauts, towel heads and slopes.

People don't hurt *people*.

Likewise, people in community don't abuse, that – as we have seen – happens in isolation. My mum grew up in a small country village in the 1930s. She said they had a blacksmith, a post office, a pub, a grocery store and a paedophile. Everyone knew which was which, it was all visible, no one went to prison or was relocated – you just kept your kids away from the old man who fiddled with children.

Pick up trash.

And if you see a hot hatch driving down the road with *KFC* or *McDonald's* containers being thrown out of the window hunt them down and kill them like dogs, and if anyone objects just say *Jerry said it was okay.*

Give money to homeless people – it doesn't matter if they *just spend it on drugs or alcohol*, they're in pain, who are you to judge? Give them some cash, you have so much more than them and they are still members of our tribe. In fact – why not go crazy! Talk to them, find out how they got there, what they need, how you can help.

Don't just walk on by – that's the road to extinction.

Take responsibility for your own evolution – you don't have to get spangled on strange jungle medicine, and you don't have to do therapy or go traipsing around old trenches or graveyards, but follow your heart, let your feelings guide you – whenever you have an awakening, pursue it, even if you don't know why.

It's trying to bring you *home.*

Late summer had come around once more, and there it was again. Not dramatic, but perceptible – that chill, I noticed it as I walked to the Tube, my skin recoiling slightly beneath my thin summer clothes, insufficient now after so many weeks of near nudity, feet constricted in unfamiliar leather, legs suffocating in cloth.

On our way back from holiday the previous day me and my kids had visited Uncle Bill's grave in a Rouen war cemetery, then to the Somme, all poppies, Roman roads and white headstones, before the unavoidable reality of dropping them back with their mum and driving home with a tan on my skin and a lump in my throat.

And now, back in the acrid metropolis I passed the man selling the *Big Issue* and the beggars who crowd the stairs to the station, descending down into the machine, the screeching clank of escalators and hot fetid air catching in my throat; shooting around this subterranean world in a tin can I wondered how we ever got to this state of madness and what would the ancients make of this thing we call progress?

This is what happens when you accept insanity.

Emerging at West Brompton like a diver coming up for air, I turned into the cemetery, no need to pause at the coffee shop by the gates – nothing to avoid now; the tan stone in my pocket pressing against my thigh I walked purposefully as if to a rendezvous with an old friend.

Burroughs used to cruise this graveyard when he lived at the Empress Hotel a short walk down the road; I could almost see him reclining on the grass amongst the tombs, all around me I could feel the ghosts, perhaps not so odd given my circumstances – there was Emmeline Pankhurst, her striking gravestone standing out amongst the decay, a fitting monument to the most amazing and courageous of women. Arrested and incarcerated on multiple occasions for her militant protests she described how – *Holloway became a place of horror and torment. Sickening scenes of violence took place almost every hour of the day, as the doctors went from cell to cell performing their hideous office.*

Time magazine named her as one of the 100 Most Important People of the 20ᵗʰ Century, stating *she shaped an idea of women for our time; she shook society into a new pattern from which there could be no going back.*

Shit has changed.

Brompton Cemetery was London District's Military Cemetery from 1854 to 1939, it's full of old soldiers, VC recipients and veterans like Charles Ellingworth who fought in both the Indian Mutiny and the Crimea as part of the infamous *Thin Red Line* at Balaclava where 500 Sutherland Highlanders broke the massed Russian cavalry. So too there are generals, colour sergeants, colonels and privates, Spitfire pilots and sailors – and whilst war cemeteries elsewhere are somewhat regimented, with its irregular and varied monuments set at jaunty angles Brompton feels more like a gathering of old comrades.

Uncle Bill's ghost too I feel; I seemed to have carried some of his essence back with me from France, the visit touching me profoundly. My grandmother spoke of him so often that her memories have become merged with my own and so it is that I can remember when he brought parrots and monkeys back from the Boer War, and how when he used to get drunk he'd crawl under the large oak table in the farmhouse kitchen and hold on to the leg and no one could shift him. Home on leave from the front I recall him promising to give my great-grandmother his soldier's kilt after the Great War as a skirt.

But of course, he never did.

Instead, he became one of my guardian angels, a fallen hero who made me feel I belonged within my family, part of a line of men I could admire and respect, who had my back and were there for me. They gave me a sense of pride in my own actions as their representative, my job to honour them and make them proud. And knowing I was *of* them somehow made it okay to be me, I understood my own wildness, my own adventurous spirit, that I carried the flame on their behalf as my children will do after I am gone.

I like cemeteries.

No one's in a rush; they're not going anywhere – they're settled. Here there is no suffering, no disease, no loneliness, no betrayal, no pain except for that which we, the living, bring – those underfoot are at peace, and why it's they we pity and not ourselves I know not... These people have completed their mission, they've lived their lives and left their mark – some more so than others, and now their demons sleep quietly beside them.

Sitting on a bench regarding the abundance of death and life, the tumble of weeds and brambles, nettles, wildflowers and grasses wild as any ocean with its shark fin gravestones slashing the surface it struck me – the divide between agony and ecstasy... is thinner *still* than a cigarette paper, this intensity of this pain that I have worked so hard to be able to feel is the blossoming of decades of psychological, psychedelic, spiritual and emotional exploration taking me higher than I imagined possible in all my psychonautical adventures, and there is indeed sweetness to suffering, the sweetness of life in *all* its intensity, pure, demented, unadulterated, intense – complete.

Somewhere along the line I can't help wondering if I made a pact with the Devil – maybe long ago in the dead of night reading an incantation to raise Pan – but as Keith Richards said, *it's not always easy to know exactly when the deal went down...*

The elemental forces I summoned that night and then awakened in an olive grove in North Africa possessed me, taking me not just to the edge of a rooftop in Tangier but to the edge of madness and beyond, the very fertility of nature at times too much to bear as that dark, potent energy coursed through my body, leaving me shaken, raw and weeping at the sheer *power* of it all.

But that's the price you pay when you agree to feel, to feel it *all*, no matter what the cost, no dumbing down of the senses nor dulling of the taste buds, bitter, sweet and everything in between, sometimes nectar, at other times bile – the juice of existence comes in all flavours.

This being human is not easy – how do we come to terms with all that we are, especially if you're born with a conscience? What other species organises itself in such a way as to invade another territory and destroy all the inhabitants? The only equivalent would be a virus. I mean it's insane when you go into it – we take members of our societies and we train and equip them to attack and kill, en masse, members of our own kind. And someone, somewhere *right now* is working away in a lab figuring out the best way to kill as many people as efficiently as possible – what other species is so cruel, so quick to murder, rape and torture?

None more so than us.

But...

How many fish have painted a Picasso?

How many of the other apes have composed an opera? A sonnet? Built a temple or an ocean-going yacht or a spaceship or a camera? Pioneered lifesaving surgery or the ability to transplant organs...

No other species, as far as we can tell, is as inquisitive, curious and creative as ours.

And is there another creature that really feels love and compassion to the extent that we do?

We have the ability to create or destroy, to love or to hate in the way that no other being can.

We have but a simple choice.

Feed the demon.

Or nurture the daimōn.

It was hot; I shrugged the French labourer's jacket from my shoulders, overhead the sky clear save for the ever-present crows and an occasional swallow plucking midges from the warm air; beside a grave stood two large abandoned suitcases, a giant teddy bear sunbathing spread-eagled on the grass, whilst in the distance I could see a man exercising two large blue parrots and so, clutching the stone in my palm...

I walked towards him.

Datta Dayadhvam Damyata
Shantih shantih shantih

Transformation

Look back over all of these enquiries. What have you learned? What was most important, what stands out?

Consolidate all of your notes and see if you can summarise in one paragraph or sentence the most important thing that you've become aware of.

Look at your life as a whole. Are you where you want to be, are you who you want to be – do you like what you've discovered?

How well do you know your demons?

How well do you know your daimōns?

Who's running the show?

Acknowledgements

Mai Hua, thank you for your boundless love, for tolerating my ego and the great many 'mantrums' that went into the making of this book and for dragging your arse around cold, wet, muddy battlefields in the depths of winter, you'd have frozen to death were it not for the huge warmth of your soul.

Next time I say, don't take ayahuasca...

Don't take ayahuasca.

So too Jonny Phillips, Steve Howse and Robin Evans.

Truly remarkable men – the strength and inspiration of your company inspired me to go on when my feet were cold and blistered and somehow, through that encounter, I found the heart of this book.

Thank you for your comradeship.

Janan Kubba, Noor Kubba Hyde and Tara Kubba Hyde for your love and support, for always believing in me and inspiring the shit out of me with your collective and individual beauty and wisdom.

Stephen Hopgood, thank you for your unfailing friendship, your guts (which I've witnessed both inside and out), for your feedback and for trawling through various drafts of the manuscript, for helping me shape it and being a part of it.

Melissa Unger for fucking this book *right* up by saying in response to some early pages – *this could be your masterpiece...*

No pressure.

Thank you for your chaos management, your friendship and constant, bottomless support.

Sebastian Junger for your generosity of spirit, wisdom, brilliance and friendship.

Tim Page, thank you for your time, friendship, for the rambling, always fascinating conversations and for being one of the few people who actually deserves the title living legend.

Will Blanchard, my oldest friend, co-conspirator and true inspiration, thank you for reading the manuscript in record time, for your uniqueness of character that showed me the way before I even knew there was a way. Love you, man.

Zoe Ereni for your encouragement, trust, humour, fighting spirit and enthusiasm – can't wait to see what you publish.

Ainhoa Púa for your distracting beauty in all that you do.

Brendan O'Byrne, I'm sorry your words got edited out, thank you for your time, warmth, trust and courage.

Stephen Mayes for your generous support from the very beginning, and Idil Ibrahim for graciously opening so many doors for me.

Charlie Taylor for your love and warmth that spans many decades and for suggesting that maybe I might possibly write this one – for the reader?

Christine Rockwell whom I've never met but who so graciously took time to read the manuscript twice and give me such fantastic notes which ultimately helped shape the book.

Pete and Alice, my maternal grandparents, for showing me how to stick it to the man.

Dedicated to the memory of Steve Annett, 1950-2019, our very own and beloved Prometheus who lived life to the full and refused to have it any other way.

The Holy Spirit's Interpretation of the New Testament
A Course in Understanding and Acceptance
Regina Dawn Akers
Following on from the strength of *A Course In Miracles*, NTI
teaches us how to experience the love and oneness of God.
Paperback: 978-1-84694-085-9 ebook: 978-1-78099-083-5

The Message of A Course In Miracles
A translation of the Text in plain language
Elizabeth A. Cronkhite
A translation of *A Course in Miracles* into plain, everyday
language for anyone seeking inner peace. The companion
volume, *Practicing A Course In Miracles*, offers practical lessons
and mentoring.
Paperback: 978-1-84694-319-5 ebook: 978-1-84694-642-4

Your Simple Path
Find Happiness in every step
Ian Tucker
A guide to helping us reconnect with what is really important in
our lives.
Paperback: 978-1-78279-349-6 ebook: 978-1-78279-348-9

365 Days of Wisdom
Daily Messages To Inspire You Through The Year
Dadi Janki
Daily messages which cool the mind, warm the heart and guide
you along your journey.
Paperback: 978-1-84694-863-3 ebook: 978-1-84694-864-0

Body of Wisdom
Women's Spiritual Power and How it Serves
Hilary Hart
Bringing together the dreams and experiences of women across
the world with today's most visionary spiritual teachers.
Paperback: 978-1-78099-696-7 ebook: 978-1-78099-695-0

Dying to Be Free
From Enforced Secrecy to Near Death to True Transformation
Hannah Robinson
After an unexpected accident and near-death experience, Hannah
Robinson found herself radically transforming her life, while a
remarkable new insight altered her relationship with her father, a
practising Catholic priest.
Paperback: 978-1-78535-254-6 ebook: 978-1-78535-255-3

The Ecology of the Soul
A Manual of Peace, Power and Personal Growth for Real People
in the Real World
Aidan Walker
Balance your own inner Ecology of the Soul to regain your
natural state of peace, power and wellbeing.
Paperback: 978-1-78279-850-7 ebook: 978-1-78279-849-1

Not I, Not other than I
The Life and Teachings of Russel Williams
Steve Taylor, Russel Williams
The miraculous life and inspiring teachings of one of the World's
greatest living Sages.
Paperback: 978-1-78279-729-6 ebook: 978-1-78279-728-9

On the Other Side of Love
A woman's unconventional journey towards wisdom
Muriel Maufroy
When life has lost all meaning, what do you do?
Paperback: 978-1-78535-281-2 ebook: 978-1-78535-282-9

Practicing A Course In Miracles
A translation of the Workbook in plain language, with mentor's
notes
Elizabeth A. Cronkhite
The practical second and third volumes of The Plain-Language
A Course In Miracles.
Paperback: 978-1-84694-403-1 ebook: 978-1-78099-072-9

Quantum Bliss
The Quantum Mechanics of Happiness, Abundance, and Health
George S. Mentz
Quantum Bliss is the breakthrough summary of success and
spirituality secrets that customers have been waiting for.
Paperback: 978-1-78535-203-4 ebook: 978-1-78535-204-1

The Upside Down Mountain
Mags MacKean
A must-read for anyone weary of chasing success and happiness
– one woman's inspirational journey swapping the uphill slog for
the downhill slope.
Paperback: 978-1-78535-171-6 ebook: 978-1-78535-172-3

Your Personal Tuning Fork
The Endocrine System
Deborah Bates
Discover your body's health secret, the endocrine system, and
'twang' your way to sustainable health!
Paperback: 978-1-84694-503-8 ebook: 978-1-78099-697-4

Readers of ebooks can buy or view any of these bestsellers by clicking on the live link in the title. Most titles are published in paperback and as an ebook. Paperbacks are available in traditional bookshops. Both print and ebook formats are available online.

Find more titles and sign up to our readers' newsletter at http://www.johnhuntpublishing.com/mind-body-spirit

Follow us on Facebook at https://www.facebook.com/OBooks/ and Twitter at https://twitter.com/obooks